I'M STUCK, YOU'RE STUCK

I'M STUCK, YOU'RE STUCK

Break Through to Better Work Relationships and Results By Discovering Your DiSC Behavioral Style

Tom Ritchey
with Alan Axelrod

Produced by Alison Brown Cerier Book Development, Inc.

An Inscape Guide

BERRETT-KOEHLER PUBLISHERS, INC.
San Francisco

Berrett-Koehler Publishers, Inc.
235 Montgomery Street, Suite 650
San Francisco, CA 94104-2916
Tel: (415) 288-0260 Fax: (415) 362-2512 www.bkconnection.com

Ordering Information

Quantity sales. Special discounts are available on quantity purchases by corporations, associations, and others. For details, contact the "Special Sales Department" at the Berrett-Koehler address above.

Individual sales. Berrett-Koehler publications are available through most bookstores. They can also be ordered direct from Berrett-Koehler: Tel: (800) 929-2929; Fax: (802) 864-7626; www.bkconnection.com

Orders for college textbook/course adoption use. Please contact Berrett-Koehler: Tel: (800) 929-2929; Fax: (802) 864-7626.

Orders by U.S. trade bookstores and wholesalers. Please contact Publishers Group West, 1700 Fourth Street, Berkeley, CA 94710. Tel: (510) 528-1444; Fax (510) 528-3444.

Printed in the United States of America

Berrett-Koehler books are printed on long-lasting acid-free paper. When it is available, we choose paper that has been manufactured by environmentally responsible processes. These may include using trees grown in sustainable forests, incorporating recycled paper, minimizing chlorine in bleaching, or recycling the energy produced at the paper mill.

DiSC is a registered trademark of Inscape Publishing, Inc.
Personal Profile System is a registered trademark of Inscape Publishing, Inc.

Library of Congress Cataloging-in-Publication Data
Ritchey, Tom, 1943-
 I'm stuck, you're stuck: break through to better work relationships and results by discovering your DiSC behavioral style / Tom Ritchey with Alan Axelrod.
  p.cm.
  ISBN-10: 1-57675-133-3; ISBN-13: 978-1-57675-133-6
  1. Communication in organizations. I. Axelrod, Alan, 1952- II. Title

 HD30.3 .R58 2001
 158.7—dc21   00—11285

First Edition
10 09 08 07 06   10 9 8 7 6 5 4 3

Cover design: Susan Malikowski, Autographix
Interior design: Michaelis/Carpelis Design Associates
Copyeditor: Andrea Chesman

Contents

Preface

*"If we only knew what we know . . .
we would be astonished at the treasures
contained in our knowledge."*
Immanuel Kant

We spend years in and out of school, striving to learn those things that could make our life a happy, successful one. We work hard to find great relationships, work we care about, and a future we can believe in. We may know exactly what we want, or we may be finding our way as we go along. Whatever path we're on, though, we often get stuck, more times than we imagined we would. Why? Because no one can get there alone. We need other people to understand us, care about us, and work with us. And we need to understand, care about, and work with others.

I started out as a teacher. I figured out early in life that I wanted to get involved in education. In the early 1970s, I taught elementary school and soon became a young principal. I was on the fast track and thought I could go full speed ahead. But it wasn't happening. I was responsible for getting results through a wide range of people, including teachers, administrators, parents, a school board, and the community. The things I'd always done that had contributed to my individual success were no longer always working. Sometimes I got stuck in first gear.

It was a time of dramatic change in public education, and everyone had a point of view. What we didn't have was good communication. Conflict was rising. My staff, parents, and administrators spent too much time pointing the finger of blame at each other, and the children were losing. I looked around at all the smart, dedicated, and frustrated people and wondered, "Now what do I do?"

I knew I had to learn a new way to understand and deal with what was happening to me and my team. Otherwise, we'd never break through the brick wall in front of us.

There's an old saying, "When the student is ready, the teacher appears." I was ready when I went to my first seminar on the DISC behavioral model. The seminar was presented by Dr. John Geier of the University of Minnesota. Dr. Geier had conducted research on the DISC model originally developed by the psychologist William Moulton Marston in the 1920s. Dr. Geier had developed a version of a simple assessment tool based on DISC that provided respondents with a personal profile of their behavioral preferences. As an educator, I was well acquainted with various psychological tests and assessments floating around academia. I was skeptical whether DISC could help experienced adults who already knew who they were and what they wanted. Fortunately, I was wrong. I learned that DISC is a theoretical model that really works.

DISC didn't put a label on me and tell me my "type." It showed me how I do things, based on my thoughts and emotions in different situations, with different people. By responding to a short set of research-based phrases, I got personalized feedback about my preferred behavioral style. I learned when my style might be a strength and, when overused, how it became a weakness. I found a quick way to get a handle on why I was responding a certain way. I also understood why others were responding differently.

Best of all, DISC focused my attention on a very basic principle of human interaction: When confronted with roadblocks, people are capable of adapting to find a way to move on—if we choose to do so.

My big DISC "a-ha!" was that being stuck is often a choice. With a little self-awareness and an appreciation of the behavioral differences of others, we can find our way out of the ruts in which we are stuck.

In discovering DISC on that lucky day nearly thirty years ago, I found a profound but simple and memorable way to help me understand why we do the things we do. I developed and conducted seminars for my staff and other professionals. We learned the common language of DISC. We used that language to communicate, in good times and bad, about how we saw things, and what we might need from others. We used the language and learning of DISC to build relationships with each other, our students, and the community.

That was just the beginning for me, however. DISC had such an impact on my life and work that I headed down a new career path: I became a training and development professional. I wanted to share DISC with a broader range of people in the private and public sectors. In the last twenty-five years I have trained thousands of people in the DISC model. For the last ten of those years, I have been president, and now chief learning officer, for Inscape Publishing, the international publisher of the original DISC assessment, the Personal Profile System®.

Inscape conducts ongoing research across diverse populations and continues refinement of the DISC model. Inscape's DISC products, trademarked as DiSC, with a small "i," have been used by more than 40 million people, in seventeen languages, in training and development seminars around the world. You can learn more about Inscape at the back of this book.

I wrote *I'm Stuck, You're Stuck* because I, along with the Inscape team, believe it's time that our research-based DiSC profile is available to everyone, whether or not your workplace training department uses DiSC.

We live in times of unprecedented change, speed, and information overload. At work, we're continuously challenged to know more, to do more, to believe speed is life. Well, speed isn't life. It may be a fact of life, but human nature tends to slow us down. Technology means faster communication, only if people are really communicating. So how do we consciously and effectively relate in a world that demands instant reaction? How do we translate this landslide of data in an increasingly global workforce into shared meaning, shared action, and shared results?

Let DiSC be the framework on which you build the skills to quickly analyze the situation, reflect on your behavior, influence your surroundings, and take positive action. I'm confident the insights you gain through DiSC will help you break through those stuck moments and stalled relationships in every part of your work life. By understanding the adaptability that waits within you, you can keep moving forward, guided by past experience to future opportunity.

Wherever you are in your journey, welcome to what I hope will be a powerful and rewarding next step for you.

Tom Ritchey
Inscape Publishing

Acknowledgments

This book is the result of a sharing of knowledge and blending of talents by a number of people. I would like to first thank Patricia Benson for her vision, creativity, and determination in getting this book done.

I would like to acknowledge William Moulton Marston for his elegant and timeless theory of DISC, and thank the following people for advancing our knowledge of DISC and self-assessments: John Geier; Dorothy Downey; Pamela Cole; Miriam Kragness, Ph.D.; and Julie Straw.

For more than two decades, thousands of trainers and consultants around the world have used Inscape's DiSC tools in their work. My thanks to each and every one of you.

I owe a great debt to Alison Brown Cerier, developer and editor, and Alan Axelrod, writer, whose talents helped channel my years of experience using DiSC into a coherent, organized text.

Lastly, I am profoundly grateful to Steve Piersanti and the staff of Berrett-Koehler for their invaluable partnership in helping us create greater access to DiSC learning through this book.

Feeling Stuck?

CHAPTER ONE

During your workday, do you sometimes feel *stuck?* Stuck with someone who's difficult to work with, no matter how hard you try? Stuck with ways of doing things that aren't getting good results? Stuck with frustration, stress, anger?

There are many ways to get stuck at work, including some you may not have thought of before.

Stuck doing things the same way over and over. We're creatures of habit. Day after day, we go about our work the way we always have. We work in ways that we find natural and comfortable, without thinking about them too much. Often we get good results, which encourages us to work in those ways again. The problem is that the usual ways don't always yield good results. Our results, or our work relationships, aren't what they should be. We expect something different to happen, but we keep doing things the same way. We're stuck!

Stuck working with someone who's "difficult." Wouldn't work be great if it weren't for all those people? Your "difficult person" may be a manager, assistant, colleague, teammate, or client. Between you there are miscommunications, misunderstandings, tension, perhaps open conflict. Over time, the two of you have started to play well-rehearsed roles. Whenever you do x, the other person does y. Both of you are dug into your positions. You're stuck.

Stuck with an assignment you don't like. Sometimes work can seem like play. The day passes quickly. You know you're working at your best. You may feel "flow"—moments when you're totally absorbed in the work. On the other hand, almost all jobs involve some tasks that really feel like work. These tasks make you feel bored, confused, frustrated, perhaps even threatened. The hands on the clock seem to be stuck—and so do you.

Stuck with people who don't want to follow your lead. Have you ever moved forward in your thinking, then looked around and realized that you were all alone? Why do the others resist change so much? Why can't they get on board? If you think other people are stuck, you're stuck, too—stuck feeling isolated, lonely, or exasperated.

Stuck assuming that other people are stuck. Actually, if you think other people are stuck, that may be part of the problem. There's an irony hidden in the title of this book, *I'm Stuck, You're Stuck:* You can't know whether the other person feels stuck since you can't climb inside another person's head. In fact, assuming you do know what someone else is thinking and feeling is one reason that situations get stuck. People can surprise you. Perhaps the other person thinks everything is fine. Perhaps the other person sees options for resolving the situation and is looking for an opening from you. By assuming that the other person is stuck, you can get stuck yourself.

Stuck thinking about yourself a certain way. People's images of themselves can get stuck, too. They think they're too successful, too experienced, too wonderful, too old, too young, too male, too female, too tired, too strong to do something differently. While it is not possible to change who you are, it is possible to change how you do things. If you are putting limitations on yourself, you can get stuck.

Think about the stuck situations in your life. How are you stuck today? Consider both situations that seem seriously stuck (hurtful, depressing) and situations that are just a little bit stuck. Small tensions, dings, and annoyances might not seem important, but they add up, and they put a constant low level of stress into your day.

"Stuck" can feel frustrating, stressful, lonely, confusing. Even the imagery surrounding the word is negative: stuck in the mud, stuck in the snow, stuck in a rut, stuck in neutral.

What Doesn't Work

Because nobody wants to feel stuck, people often try to get unstuck.

Some people assume the stuck situation is their fault. They try harder, but nothing improves. They might look for a class, seminar, or book to help them figure out what needs to change.

Many more people assume that it's the other person's fault. They might try pleading, nagging, or bribing, but it's even harder to change someone else than it is to change yourself.

There are lots of ways people try to get unstuck from assignments they don't care for. Some people procrastinate, others delegate. Some develop selective hearing—what they don't hear, they don't have to deal with. Some people just walk away from a stuck situation.

Some people who feel very stuck go job-hunting. Sometimes a new job is a good idea, but there are difficult people and difficult tasks wherever you go.

None of these approaches really works.

The Way You See It

The usual ways to overcome stuck situations don't work because people try to change themselves or other people. That isn't realistic.

It's far more realistic and effective to change something else: *the way you see the situation.*

A situation becomes stuck because you can't see it clearly anymore. You can't see what is really happening, and you can't see how the situation could possibly change.

Situations become fuzzy because emotions are attached to them. Have you ever been so angry that you literally saw red? When people become enraged, there are physical changes in the eye, so it seems they're looking through a red fog. Peripheral vision narrows, too. *They don't see as well as they usually do.* You don't have to get over-the-top angry for your judgment to be clouded. Lower-level conflict can blur your vision, too.

Miscommunications and conflicts seem very personal. When someone is arguing, complaining, whining, and venting, what you see is the grimace, the groans, the shouts, the shaking head, the pointing finger. Soon you may be doing the same. If that's not your style, you might grow quiet and withdrawn, but you're still angry inside. At this point, no one's seeing the issues clearly. Everyone has blurry vision.

Picture your stuck situation as a jagged mountain range with lots of sharp rocks and dangerous places. Now the fog has descended, and you can't see a pass that would take you through the range, safe into the valley on the other side.

Through this book, you can discover passes through the mountain range of your situation. You will clear away the fog and see the situation clearly. You will start where you are and find paths to where you want to be.

A Tool Called DiSC

All mountain explorers need dependable equipment. On your journey, your tool will be DiSC. This self-discovery tool will help you see the situation in new ways, with new options.

DiSC is a tool you can depend on to be accurate and field-tested. DiSC has been researched and refined for more than twenty years. It has been used across North America and has been translated and validated for people in many other countries. Thousands of companies and organizations, big and small, have used DiSC. Trainers and consultants have used DiSC in workshops attended by more than 40 million people worldwide.

DiSC began with a theory of human behavior first advanced in the 1920s by the American psychologist William Moulton Marston. Marston was interested in how normal people felt and behaved as they interacted with the world around them. Based on his pioneering research, Marston developed a model of behavior that identified four distinct behavioral dimensions. In 1972, Inscape Publishing, a Minneapolis-based research and publishing firm, used Marston's work as the foundation for further research, which resulted in the Personal Profile System, a learning instrument that gave people unprecedented access to an understanding of their own feelings and behavior in almost any situation. Inscape Publishing has continued to refine and improve the Personal Profile System through ongoing research, using thousands of

The Research behind DiSC

A learning instrument like DiSC can provide useful feedback only if *it measures what it claims to measure (validity) and if it does so consistently (reliability).* Many instruments, though often used by good companies, lack even minimal validity and reliability. In contrast, Inscape Publishing uses research to ensure that our instruments provide you with accurate and meaningful information.

When research specialists assess how good an instrument is, they first consider the sample population. If the sample were white male accountants from Kansas, then the instrument would only be appropriate for use by white male accountants from Kansas. Inscape Publishing makes sure that our research samples are representative of people of different ages and racial backgrounds and from a wide variety of occupations and geographical locations.

Instruments also have to be reliable, which means the results are consistent. Professional-quality instruments offer "scale reliability" greater than .70. The numbers for Inscape's DiSC range from .77 to .85.

A high-quality behavioral instrument also offers validity, in other words, *it measures what it is said to measure.* Validity was emphasized in creating both the scales and the response pattern feedback. The validity of the Inscape's DiSC scales has been confirmed by two types of statistical analyses, one called factor analysis and the other called multidimensional scaling.

For more details and guidelines for appropriate use, see "The Research behind DiSC" at the end of the book.

demographically and professionally diverse respondents. This book is the first time Inscape's DiSC instrument has been available outside of the professional training and development environment.

Inscape's DiSC instrument is a highly reliable way to gain insight into your thoughts, feelings, and behavior— not just in an abstract, theoretical way, but in specific, real-world situations.

Points of View

DiSC is based on the assumption that you are the expert on you.

Using DiSC is like looking in a mirror. Have you ever looked at your face in a mirror and discovered something? You asked yourself: "What is going on with that hair?" The hair "situation" was there all along, but you hadn't noticed it yet. The mirror helped you notice.

When you look in the mirror, what you see depends on your point of view. You might think your body looks chubby, but someone else might say you look just fine. People who have recently lost a lot of weight might think they look great even if they're still overweight according to a doctor's weight tables. What people see in the mirror depends on their point of view.

How much gray is in your hair? How many wrinkles? Mustache working, or not? Earrings too much? Depends on your point of view.

The DiSC tool is based on the fact that there are distinct ways to look at any situation. Here's a story about four people and four points of view.

One Monday morning, the president of a small publishing company called four managers to a meeting. There was Mary Jane, the take-charge acquisitions editor; Bill, the ever-enthusiastic sales manager; Max, the reliable production manager; and Wanda, the letter-perfect copy editor.

The president said, "I have an exciting announcement to make."

Mary Jane drummed on the table with her fingers.

"That's great!" said Bill.

Max smiled politely.

Wanda looked worried.

"I'm bringing in a consultant—a top person—to look over our operations from top to bottom and give us a new perspective on what we're doing, what we're doing right, and what we could be doing better. He—"

"Well, there are a number of things I want to tell this 'consultant,'" Mary Jane interrupted. "It takes a lot to make a good deal these days."

"It would be great to have someone new to bounce some ideas off of," said Bill.

"Look," Wanda said, pushing her chair back from the table, "I don't want someone to come in here and tell *me* how to do *my* job. How long will this person be here? What, exactly, will this person want to know? And what—exactly— will I have to do?"

"People, people, relax! He's not even here yet. Max, we haven't heard from you."

"Well, I'll go along with whatever you and the others want. I'll certainly listen to whatever this man has to say. But I sure hope he doesn't go making changes right and left."

The president left the meeting puzzled that everyone wasn't as excited as he was. He didn't realize that each person saw the consultant's visit differently.

People have different points of view on "opportunities." They also have different points of view on:

- rules
- competition
- working alone
- working on a team
- fact-checking
- problems
- schmoozing
- deadlines
- chaos
- praise
- helping others
- criticism
- getting input
- responsibility
- decision-making
- stability
- standards
- rapid change
- and many other common work situations

DiSC helps you get in touch with your own point of view. In any given situation, how are you thinking, feeling, and behaving?

If You Were More Like Me, We Wouldn't Have This Problem

When presented with an opportunity or challenge, we tend to behave in ways shaped by our points of view. Others may see things very differently from the way we do, and may therefore behave in very different ways. It's part of the human condition. We are all products—and sometimes, prisoners—of our particular point of view. Often, misunderstandings, compromised results, out-and-out conflict, or just vaguely muffled, unsatisfactory outcomes are not matters of simple right or wrong, but of differing points of view.

Have you experienced any of these situations?

- You had to work on a team, but you wanted to work solo on the project.
- You looked at a problem and saw what needed to be done but couldn't get anybody to change the status quo.
- You think schmoozing pays off in the long run, but your performance review was critical of the time you spend socializing.
- Other people seemed excited about the transitional period, but it felt chaotic to you.
- You prepared a wonderfully detailed status report, but your boss cut you off in the middle of presenting it.
- You're tired of everybody telling you how to do your job.

These are common complaints, the rules rather than the exceptions. One way or another, they arise from conflicts, perceived or actual, or *the fear of conflicts,* between your point of view and the points of view of others.

Does this mean that we are all doomed to conflict and collide or to miss one another completely? Can we never connect in a productive way? Will we fail to grasp one opportunity after another? Are we destined to be disappointed? Will situation after situation keep getting stuck?

There is a better way.

First, accept yourself, and accept others. Different isn't necessarily bad—it's just different. Try to be grateful for what others may be bringing to the situation. Of course, it's hard to be grateful when the differences are causing relationship stress.

Transforming conflict into strength does not require changing who you are, but it does require that you understand your own point of view: *why* you respond and feel and behave the way you do. Once you understand your point of view, it becomes much easier to understand those of others.

When you understand and accept your point of view and the points of view of others, you'll see the situation in a whole new way, with new options for you.

Other Sources of Stuck

DiSC can help you improve many situations that have become stuck, but like all approaches, it can't fix them all. Not all stuck situations are caused by different points of view. Some situations become stuck because of:

Personal prejudices. In other words, making judgments about a group of people based on observations of one person who happens to belong to that group can cause a situation to become stuck. Someone has made assumptions based on age, dress, race, ethnicity, gender, or sex. There are also workplace prejudices based on job titles and positions (for example, making assumptions about everyone in marketing or everyone in engineering). In today's diverse world, if you don't look at each person as an individual, you can get stuck.

Different values. In other words, the rules by which people live their lives can be different and lead to conflict. DiSC doesn't reveal personal value systems (what people believe is important). If two people have strongly held and conflicting values, a situation between them can get stuck.

Lack of resources. Sometimes there is not enough people, money, or knowledge to get the job done. Is everyone overworked? Does the organization lack people with the right skills or experience? Are there structural or organizational problems? A situation can get stuck because the organization isn't providing the resources to resolve it.

While DiSC doesn't make issues like these go away, it can help diffuse the emotions that often surround them. The process of using DiSC tends to move people from judging to understanding and respecting, which can improve any situation. Also, many people have found that when one stuck situation is resolved, other situations get unstuck, too. By fixing the small issues, you just might fix a seemingly intractable one.

Taking Yourself off Automatic Pilot

The most important message of this book is this: Take yourself off automatic pilot. Stop doing things the same way over and over, without thinking about it. Step back from the situation. Stop and reflect. DiSC makes this simple and quick.

You don't live and work in a vacuum. So if you're going to get unstuck, you need to act in ways that will meet the needs of both yourself and other people. DiSC helps you view the situation from different perspectives.

DiSC begins with self-awareness, but it doesn't end there. It also develops "other-awareness" and "situation-awareness." DiSC is about self, other, and situation: SOS. You might say, it's not about me and it's not about you; it's about us.

While you are considering ways you might act on what you learn, think small. Usually the best way to move forward is to take baby steps. Often if you take a baby step toward someone else, that person will take a big step toward you. If you move a little, often you won't have to move farther. Before you can take a step, though, you need to know in which direction to go. You need to take in some data, and that's where DiSC comes in.

Start with one problem. Focus on one stuck situation and work on that. Often other problems will go away, too.

Wonderful things will happen when you take yourself off automatic pilot.

Taking DiSC

During the Cold War, radio and TV programs were regularly interrupted by the solemn announcement that the Emergency Broadcasting System was conducting a test: "THIS IS A TEST," a baritone voice intoned. "THIS IS ONLY A TEST."

Well, the Cold War is over, and the other good news is that what you are about to be offered is NOT A TEST.

After years of testing by schools and employers, it's understandable that many people tense up the minute they hear the word "test." This is not a test. You can't pass or fail it. Nor does it predict success or failure. You won't grade it, and no one else will either.

It's not a test; it's a tool. While tests are graded by others so they can "see how you're doing," the DiSC tool is about *you* and for *you*, to help you make the choices that will bring the results you want.

So relax.

Picking a Focus

The first step—a key one—is to choose a focus. You will take DiSC while holding a specific situation in your mind. You will focus on a real time, a real place, a real person, a real problem, a real project, a real issue. That way, you'll be able to apply what you learn in a specific context.

Focus on your real life. You can focus on a stuck situation or on any other situation that you would like to investigate—even one that is enjoyable. Think in terms of a real time, a real place, a real person, a real problem, a real project, a real issue. Think about how you are feeling, thinking, and acting in a situation at work that is:

- related to a specific project, or
- with a specific person, or
- with a specific team or group, or
- with a certain customer or client, or
- concerning a specific problem or difficulty.

Before sitting down to take DiSC, take a breath and clear your mind. Then *think about yourself in a specific situation* that is important to you. The more specific and more important, the sharper your focus will be. Don't settle for a general statement. Don't make a wish, as if you're about to blow out the birthday candles ("I wish I were more successful"). Don't ask a question, as if you were getting ready to break open up a fortune cookie ("Will I get a raise?").

Instead, look at what's happening in your life now. Focus on a specific situation that matters to you *now*.

A well-defined focus includes a person or people, a place, and a time. The more details you can conjure up about your experience, the better.

Then sum up the highlights in a brief sentence and write it down. A short focus will be easy to remember and repeat to yourself. Otherwise, it's hard to keep the focus in your mind.

DiSC is about you in a specific situation, not *the* situation, but *a* situation—one of the many you find yourself in. In an hour, a day, a week, a month, choose another focus—another situation—write that one down, hold that one in your mind and imagination, and take the instrument again. DiSC is designed to be taken over and over, whenever you want to see a situation more clearly.

Instructions

On the next two pages you will find phrases. How well does each one describe how you are feeling and behaving in the situation on which you are focusing? Select the number from 1 to 5 that best indicates how accurately or inaccurately each phrase describes your feelings, thoughts, and behavior in this situation.

Write the number in the box following the phrase. Be sure to respond to every phrase. It is very important to use the full range of numbers—1, 2, 3, 4, or 5. The value—to you—of your responses is directly related to how precisely you can weight each response.

Your first response to the phrase will be the most accurate one. Go with your gut response. This is a case in which first impressions are best. Most people finish in less than ten minutes.

You may think at first that some statements don't apply, but the instrument is designed so that the phrases are related in some way to almost every situation. Be sure to respond to each one.

Working across the four columns on both pages, write after each phrase the number that best describes you in this situation. 1 = Very inaccurate, or does not apply 2 = Inaccurate 3 = Neither accurate nor inaccurate 4 = Accurate 5 = Very accurate

good listener		want to make the rules	
put up with things I don't like		go straight ahead with projects	
willing to follow orders		act in a forceful way	
will go along with others		want to win	
think of others before I decide		will be the first to act	
willing to help		do not give in	
understand others' feelings		people see me as powerful	
nice to other people		sure of myself	
have warm feelings for people		want to be in charge	
let others lead		like to take action	
don't like to cause problems		quick to act	
don't make demands of people		feel strong	
Total column 1		**Total column 2**	
Subtract	-1	Add	+2
Score	●	Score	▪

like to do things accurately		wide variety of friends	
like doing things the right way		liked by others	
do things right the first time		like to meet people	
think of what makes sense		fun to be with	
like to be precise		see things positively	
shy with others		feel contented	
good at analyzing things		happy and carefree	
think things through		liven things up	
keep things to myself		feel relaxed most of the time	
think things over carefully		happy most of the time	
don't like too much attention		find it easy to meet strangers	
don't say much in a group		communicate in a lively manner	
Total column 3		**Total column 4**	
	+0	Subtract	-2
Score	☾	Score	◈

Scoring

You have some symbols—a circle, rectangle, crescent, and diamond—matched with numbers. Each symbol corresponds to one of the four DiSC dimensions:

- ● stands for S: Supportiveness
- ▪ stands for D: Dominance
- ◖ stands for C: Conscientiousness
- ◆ stands for I: Influence

Each of these dimensions is associated with certain ways of thinking, feeling, and acting in a situation, and we'll be exploring them alone and in combination.

Add up the scores in each column, if you haven't done so already; adjust the scores by adding or subtracting as shown, and you'll have your scores for each dimension.

Why these particular phrases? The phrases in the DiSC tool have come from ongoing research, and their meaning has been validated and fine-tuned many times, using a broad sample of people of all ages and backgrounds, in a wide variety of situations, and in a range of businesses and professions.

The columns are in the order S, D, C, and I. Since we'll be talking about DiSC, not SDCI, let's unscramble your score now. Write your adjusted score for each dimension on the blank lines.

Your DiSC Score			
_____	_____	_____	_____
▪	◆	●	◖
D	I	S	C

Your Highest Dimension

Find the letter—D, I, S, or C—with the highest score. This is your highest DiSC dimension of behavior in the situation on which you have focused. Jump to the description of your highest DiSC dimension of behavior; then read about the others. It is important that you look at your highest dimension first, but it is also important to read about them all, both so you understand other people's behavior, and so you can see the full range of behavioral responses which you might use.

Dominance

If your highest total was D, the Dominance style, you tend to be strong-willed and strong-minded *in the situation you have chosen as your focus.* You also probably behave in most of the following ways in this situation:

- You don't like to let anything get in the way of achieving your goals.
- You are decisive.
- You may be impatient over how long it takes others to get going.
- You don't like to give in to the objections of others.
- You prefer making your own rules rather than being told what to do.
- You tend to be very direct, saying what's on your mind even if it's negative.
- You are competitive, and you love to win.

Influence

If your highest number was the I dimension, you probably find it rewarding to be with other people. In this situation:

- You are enthusiastic.
- You love to talk.

- You enjoy participation and group activity.
- You enjoy being on a team.
- You focus on the positive; the glass is not half empty, but half full.
- You are cheerful most of the time.
- You are expressive, outgoing, demonstrative.
- You are a "people person."

Supportiveness

If your highest dimension was S, you are likely looking for ways to be helpful in the situation you have chosen as your focus. In addition:

- You think it is important to be fair and reasonable.
- You may find it difficult to adapt to change, but once you understand that changes are necessary, you are likely to give your full support.
- You prefer to preserve what you have rather than taking a chance.
- It is usually important to you that you fit in.
- You don't like conflict.
- Although you work well in a group, you prefer to be working behind the scenes.
- Rather than argue, you probably will let other people have their way.

Conscientiousness

If your C score was highest in the focus situation, you are probably highly concerned with doing things right. For example:

- You think carefully and clearly about tasks.
- You are detail oriented.

- You plan ahead.
- You make few errors.
- You set high standards and find it rewarding to exceed them.
- You prefer to work alone or only with those whom you thoroughly trust.
- You are unhappy if you fall short of your standards.

Identifying Your DiSC Pattern

So far you have discovered your most prominent style of behavior in your focus situation, and you have begun to learn about that style. You've also read the lists describing the other three styles. Did you see something of yourself in the other styles? You probably did, because while you have only one highest score, you probably marked phrases that characterize other dimensions, too. You are multidimensional.

Let's take the interpretation of your DiSC results to the next level and find your DiSC response pattern, the combination of high scores that will more closely describe your response to the situation.

If the total for any of the four dimensions is 44 or higher, then that dimension is helping to define your response pattern in this situation.

How Common?

Among the diverse sample population on which the instrument was developed, these percentages represent the number of people who had a highest score of each dimension.

D	25%
I	23%
S	16%
C	24%
Tied	12%

DiSC at a Glance

D (Dominance)
- Getting immediate results
- Taking action
- Accepting challenges
- Making decisions quickly
- Questioning the status quo
- Solving problems

I (Influence)
- Contacting people
- Verbalizing
- Generating enthusiasm
- Entertaining people
- Viewing people and situations optimistically
- Participating in a group

S (Supportiveness)
- Performing in a consistent, predictable way
- Showing patience
- Wanting to help others
- Showing loyalty
- Being a good listener
- Creating a stable, harmonious work environment

C (Conscientiousness)
- Paying attention to key directives and standards
- Concentrating on key details
- Weighing pros and cons
- Checking for accuracy
- Analyzing performance critically
- Using a systematic approach

Look back at your totals after scoring the DiSC instrument. In the box below, write all the scores that are equal to or higher than 44. Record them in order, with the highest score first. The cutoff number is absolute. Don't count as high a dimension that's just shy of the cutoff. Write the letter for that dimension under the score. This is your DiSC Response Pattern.

Your DiSC Response Pattern				
Score 44 or above, starting with highest				
Dimension				

Five kinds of results are possible:

1. a single pattern consisting of one high dimension
2. a double combination, with the totals for two behavioral styles exceeding the cutoff
3. a triple combination, in which three styles exceed the cutoff
4. no high scores
5. all high scores

DiSC combination patterns, the doubles and triples, combine aspects of two or three styles in fascinating ways. The combinations are not a matter of simple addition, like piling one building block on top of another. They're more like baking a cake; you mix separate ingredients and end up with something new.

Note that a high score can be just over the cutoff number or it may be *way* over that number. If the score is really high for a particular dimension, you'll probably find that the description of that dimension feels even more like you!

If All Your Scores Are above the Cutoff Number

If all four of your scores are above the cutoff number, the situation you have chosen as your focus may be one in which you feel that you need to be all things to all people. You can satisfy all of the people some of the time, and some of the people all of the time, but can you really satisfy all of the people all of the time? Take DiSC again, this time being true to yourself.

Another explanation for four high dimensions is that you believe you were *supposed* to respond in a certain way, whether you really felt that way or not, so you rated almost all of the phrases as "accurate" or "very accurate." Take the instrument again (there is an extra copy at the back of the book), either focusing more closely on this situation or choosing a new one. Slow down. Think carefully about

How Common?

Among the sample population, the following percentages represent the number of people who had each response pattern. The numbers don't add up to 100 because some people had no scores above the cutoff number of 44, or all scores above the cutoff. As you can see, most people had a double or triple response pattern.

D	6%	SI	3%
I	2%	IS	4%
S	3%	IC	1%
C	7%	SC	12%
DI	3%	DIS	7%
ID	6%	IDC	5%
DS	1%	DSC	5%
DC	8%	ISC	12%

each phrase. Above all: *Use the full range of responses.*

If None of Your Scores Is above the Cutoff Number

If none of your scores is above the cutoff number, it is likely that the situation you have chosen is difficult for you to keep in focus. Retake the instrument, this time focusing more closely on the situation or choosing a new one. There is no deadline for completing the instrument, so give yourself enough time to think carefully about each phrase. Use the full range of responses.

It is also possible that you skipped some phrases, or you may have thought that some of the phrases do not apply to

Technicalities

Why adjust the totals by adding or subtracting? Why is the cutoff 44, and not 43 or 45? Because this is how the assessment is constructed. Researchers and psychologists built the DiSC tool so that the results are accurate and reliable. If you want to learn more about the technical underpinnings of the model, and about the research behind it, turn to the back of the book for "The Research behind DiSC."

GETTING ON A CROWDED ELEVATOR

- **D RESPONSE: PUSH THE "CLOSE DOOR" BUTTON THREE TIMES.**

- **I RESPONSE: TELL THE CROWD THAT'S WAITING, "COME ON IN, THERE'S ALWAYS ROOM FOR ONE MORE!"**

- **S RESPONSE: AFTER LOOKING IN AND SEEING THAT THE ELEVATOR IS FULL, TAKE THE STAIRS.**

- **C RESPONSE: CHECK THE WEIGHT LIMIT, DO SOME QUICK CALCULATIONS, AND IF THERE ARE THREE TOO MANY PEOPLE, ASK THEM TO GET OFF.**

your situation. Check over the instrument to make certain that you haven't skipped anything, and remember that the instrument is designed so that the phrases apply in *some way* to any situation.

In the next chapter, you can explore further what your response pattern means, and what it doesn't mean.

What Do Your Results Mean?

CHAPTER THREE

What you have just taken is not a personality test. DiSC does not tell you your personality "type."

Personality begins with a unique genetic makeup and forms as a person has life experiences. Personality is our hardwiring. It has many facets; for example, some people are extroverted, and some are introverted, and they always will be. We don't get to choose our personalities. They come out of how we were brought up, what we were taught in school, our experiences, and the mental and emotional equipment our genes set us up with. There are a number of instruments for measuring personality. Most widely known is the Myers-Briggs Type Indicator. You can discover your personality type, but you cannot change it.

Beyond Types

DiSC does not reveal your core personality type. Instead, it reveals how your personality is responding to your environment. Personality is, at most, half of the equation. The other half is the situation. Personality and situation interact and produce thoughts, feelings, and behaviors.

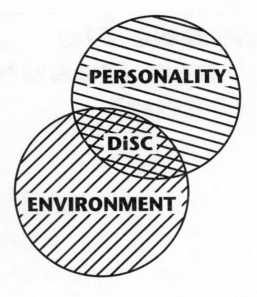

Picture two circles that are overlaping. One is the environment, the other the personality. DiSC lives where the circles overlap. DiSC describes what happens when the personality encounters the environment. You look out at the environment from the psychological home of your personality, and the way you think, feel, and act is your response—your DiSC response. Your emotional response to the environment triggers everything.

DiSC is not psychotherapy, and it won't reveal the mysteries of your inner being. But then, many situations call for immediate action, not long-term analysis. DiSC can help you take appropriate action to meet the needs of the situation and everyone involved.

While you can't change your personality, you can choose to change the way you respond to situations. That difference makes DiSC a practical tool.

The Two Questions

The four basic DiSC responses originate in two key questions that people subconsciously ask themselves when they look at a situation:

- Is this situation favorable or unfavorable to me?
- Do I have power or control in this situation?

When you took DiSC in the last chapter, did you feel that your focus situation was favorable or unfavorable? A favorable situation seems comfortable. An unfavorable situation is challenging.

Let's say you were feeling respected and trusted. The people and the setting were familiar, and things were going well generally. You felt at ease. You felt among friends. You were comfortable. It was a *favorable* environment.

If the situation was a confrontation with your boss, you probably felt that the environment was decidedly not favorable. Anytime you feel as though you're in an *unfavorable* environment, you will feel on guard. You'll feel ill at ease. You may be challenged or criticized. A situation can also feel uncomfortable if it's new to you.

Whether the situation was favorable or unfavorable, did you feel that you had the ability to control or change it? In other words, how much power did you have there?

How you read a situation is reflected in your highest DiSC dimension:

- People who believe that the environment is not favorable, but that they can control or change it, are likely to use the Dominance style of behavior.
- People who feel that the environment is favorable, and that they can control or change it, are likely to use the Influence style.
- People who feel that the environment is favorable, but that they lack power, are likely to use the Supportiveness style.
- People who feel that the environment is not favorable, and that they lack power, are likely to use the Conscientiousness style.

Here's how this plays out. A person responding with a high-D dimension looks at the environment and sees challenges to be overcome but thinks he or she can meet them. This person is seeing himself or herself as being more powerful than the environment.

A high-I response reflects optimism. Not only does this person think the situation is good, but he or she is confident in his or her ability to influence others to see things in a certain way (in other words, this person has power here).

The S response happens when someone wants to keep the environment favorable by being cooperative, supportive, and agreeable.

People tend to use the C style when they feel the situation isn't favorable for them and, moreover, that they have little influence or power in it. Sound grim? Well, it isn't. People responding with a high C aren't necessarily unhappy. They see a challenge, and they want to meet it by working within the system. They think that rules, procedures, and guidelines will ensure accuracy and quality in a world that is difficult to change.

These views of self and environment are not profound psychological or philosophical burdens that we carry around. They are just responses to specific situations.

QUICK DISC

Because your feelings about the environment and your power in it are the underpinnings of the style of behavior you choose for any situation, it is often revealing to step back from any situation and ask yourself:

▷ Does this environment feel favorable or unfavorable?
▷ Can I control or change the situation?

- **A PERSON RESPONDING AS A D IS ASKING: WHAT?**
- **A PERSON RESPONDING AS AN I IS ASKING: WHO?**
- **A PERSON RESPONDING AS AN S IS ASKING: HOW?**
- **A PERSON RESPONDING AS A C IS ASKING: WHY?**

Different Situations, Different Responses

Change the situation, and the same person may well show a different pattern of behavior.

For example, Krystal took DiSC while focusing on two different situations that year after year were important parts of her job as director of sales and marketing. The first situation was planning an annual sales conference attended by more than five hundred people from around the world. For several months before the conference, Krystal was absorbed in planning this major event. She was responsible for the keynote speakers, dozens of concurrent workshops, food and beverages on-site, sales awards, and much more. When she focused on her behavior in staff meetings during that time, she saw that her D was sky high. She was doing what was needed to get the job done. No chitchat. She was decisive, even bossy.

She then focused on how she felt, thought, and acted once the event started. Knowing that everything was in place, she switched to a role of speaking at the general sessions, presenting workshops, and schmoozing at the social events. Her I response soared. She sparkled.

Here's how another person described the different results of two times she took DiSC.

"At a meeting where I believed in the strategy we were following, I found that I was responding with a high S. I enjoyed facilitating the meeting. I made sure everyone had a chance to talk. I supported people's ideas and summarized them for the group. I wanted to help my teammates draw on their creativity and wisdom and work with them to reach our common goal.

"On another day, though, I was in a meeting where I disagreed with the course we were taking. In fact, I thought it was vital we go a different way. I pulled out my D-ness. I was loud and clear that we were making a mistake. I was far less interested in hearing other people's ideas than in getting my points across. I even interrupted them. I was bold. I wasn't interested in group dynamics. I wanted to take the lead and define our next course of action."

Multidimensional You

When you take DiSC repeatedly, different responses are possible because you have different possibilities built in to yourself.

Whether your DiSC response pattern was a single, double, or triple, you had some scores for the other dimensions, too. That is because you are not a one-dimensional being. Your responses show aspects of all the DiSC styles—but at different levels.

Here's a way to picture this. A good sound system might have a graphic equalizer, with sliders to adjust each frequency to suit the listener's taste and the acoustic environment. The listener can boost the bass frequencies, tone down the middle frequencies, and give a little kick to the higher frequencies. Picture your DiSC results as a graphic equalizer board, with a slider for each dimension. In a particular situation, one or more dimensions are turned up higher than the others; they identify the high dimension.

The others are at lower levels, but still present. With a graphic equalizer, even if you turn one slider all the way up, and the others all the way down, you never completely eliminate the other frequencies. You'll hear very heavy bass, but you'll still hear some treble and middle tones. It's the same with DiSC. One or two or three dimensions are way up high, but the others are still there. They are part of your response, too. They are your "overtones and undertones."

In music, overtones and undertones give instruments their distinctive sounds. Compare their sounds to that made by a tuning fork. Some people might say the tuning fork is not really an instrument because it can play only one note, but that's also true of a triangle or bell or even a bass drum. These are one-note instruments that can be found in any orchestra. The tuning fork is different because its tone is pure, simple, clean, constant, and, therefore, boring. The tuning-fork tone has no overtones or undertones.

Human beings are much more like violins and trombones than they are like tuning forks. Even people who routinely sound a single dominant note in their behavior—a D, an I, an S, or a C—are really a blend of all of these styles. Depending on circumstances, the ratio of one style to another may change; the blend may be temporarily higher in one style than in another. Yet it would be almost impossible to find a combination of person and situation that produces a tuning-fork pure D or I or S or C. Overtones and undertones are almost always present.

Good thing, too. Imagine your favorite music performed by a group of tuning forks. If human behavior were a case of push-this-button, get-this-response (and only this response), we would be robots rather than human beings. We are all at least somewhat unpredictable, spontaneous,

Why small "i"?

Has it been bugging you that the letter "i" in DiSC is small? That's a C response! In fact, DiSC-takers who score high on C have been known to cross out the small "i" and write in a capital letter! The small "i" originated with a proofreader who could have used a bit more C. The first Inscape DiSC instrument went to the printer with a typo, a small "i." Users liked the small letter, though, and thought it made the word more readable, memorable, and distinct. Inscape trademarked its DiSC with a small "i" and it's been DiSC ever since.

imaginative, flexible, and creative. We are instruments with many overtones and undertones.

The next time you take DiSC, a different dimension may be tuned up high. The dimension is inside you, and another situation may draw it out.

The undertones also build flexibility into your responses. These are resources you may choose to draw on when you're trying to understand other people or find solutions to problems.

What do the low levels in your response mean—those numbers lower than 44? Whether you have one, two, or three high dimensions in your response pattern, one or more of the dimensions are under the cutoff. When you took the instrument, you were asked whether or not a series of statements applied to your thoughts, feelings, and behaviors in the situation. If you scored low on a dimension, the situation might not call for that dimension, so the specific phrases didn't seem relevant. That doesn't mean that you are showing the opposite of that dimension. For example, someone who is not high in D isn't necessarily indirect or indecisive. That person is just not describing himself or herself as more direct or decisive in this situation.

One place where the tuning fork is welcome is in a physics classroom. The teacher can strike a tuning fork and hold it near a microphone attached to an oscilloscope, which will translate the sound wave into a visual image. The students see a pure and simple curve that can be expressed by a single equation. Much more complicated wave patterns would be produced by a violin, a clarinet, or, most complex of all, the human voice. The students would really struggle if they had to do a mathematical analysis of those waves! The overtones and undertones are creative, exciting, and mighty pretty—but how do you study them, talk about them?

Similarly, if you had to analyze every dimension of your DiSC responses, it might well be overwhelming. Fortunately, DiSC identifies the dimensions playing the strongest roles, singly or in combination. By zeroing in on the highest dimensions, you can get a quick handle on what's going on.

Taking It Again and Again

The DiSC instrument is designed to be taken repeatedly, whenever you feel the need to get in touch with the expert on you—who is none other than *you.* Consider taking it whenever you are facing an important decision or critical situation, and when you feel stuck. To find out how you can experience DiSC on-line or in other paper versions visit www.inscapepublishing.com.

Over time, you may find that your responses are remarkably similar from one situation to the next. On the other hand, a different focus may produce significantly different results. In the first case, you might conclude that certain

DiSC dimensions of behavior are consistently strong in you. In the second case, you might conclude that your behavior depends highly on the situation in which you happen to find yourself. For most of us, *both* are true. There are patterns, but the situation does make a difference.

If you see similar responses from situation to situation, you're seeing your "psychological home," the place you tend to return to again and again.

While some people may consistently use one style in a wide variety of situations, the instrument is still describing their thoughts, feelings, and behavior in particular situations. The DiSC instrument doesn't identify something permanent about them. That something permanent—an unchanging set of traits that shape behavior—would be the personality.

As you use DiSC over time, it will become more and more valuable to you. Like all learning, DiSC learning happens most deeply over time. Go back and review your first impressions. Did your strategies work? What would you do differently next time?

The Labeling Trap

DiSC is so simple and so direct that it is easy to misinterpret the information it provides as a picture of a permanent reality. The truth is that reality is always on the move, in a multitude of directions all at once. DiSC is a snapshot of reality, a slice of time.

Life is about change. Events—important events—whiz by in a blur. DiSC is a camera loaded with high-speed film. It takes a clear snapshot of life as it rushes by, so that you can study it. It can help you do business, make decisions, and advise and offer leadership compellingly and effectively. It helps not by changing you or changing anyone else, but by bringing your wants and needs and those of others into sharper focus—at least for the time being.

However, if you start thinking of DiSC results as permanent, you'll be tempted to assign labels to yourself and others. While reality is ever-changing, labels stick. You start seeing labels instead of people.

A label can become a convenient excuse for giving up on communication or for giving up on making an important relationship work.

"Look, I'm a D, he's a C. We just can't get along."

If we were robots, or chemical substances, or mathematical equations, a statement like this could be true. But we are human beings, multidimensional and ever-evolving.

DiSC is situational. It measures your thoughts, feelings, and behaviors as you respond to a particular situation. You might well respond differently in a different place or time. Others might, too.

So don't stick labels on yourself or other people. You're not a D, I, S, or C. You are responding to a situation in a D, I, S, or C way. You are more than a letter.

No Right and No Wrong

All four DiSC styles are valid and valuable for business and for life. The idea is to choose how you can best use your strengths and how you can most effectively communicate those strengths to others.

A consultant once did a DiSC-based workshop for managers and supervisors in a glass-construction company, a very high-C, high-D environment with lots of forceful, assertive, and analytical people. However, one of the first-level foremen in this company usually had a high-S pattern. About midway through the workshop, the consultant went around the table and asked the people what they had learned that would be important to them. And this guy, nearly in tears, answered, "You know, I learned something really important. It's okay to be me."

That's what DiSC brings to a lot of people: That it's okay to be who you are. This foreman learned that as a high-S person in many situations, he brought a lot of important qualities to the job.

Getting the Most from Your Profile
Through the next four chapters, you'll get to know the four primary DiSC styles in greater depth, including:

- strengths a person with this response style brings to the situation
- ways other people may misunderstand the response
- insights the person might choose to share with others
- common "stuck situations" and options to consider

No matter what your pattern—single, double, or triple—it's important to read all four chapters. You'll encounter people who use all these styles. Also, you have some level of each style within you, and it might well come out in a different situation in the future.

At the back of the book, there are complete descriptions of each combination response pattern: the doubles and triples. If you have a combination response, after you read the four chapters on the single dimensions, go next to the section about your combination. It's not useful—and can be confusing—to read about all the combination patterns now. Later, though, you might want to read some of the combination patterns that are very different from your own to broaden your understanding of how other people might respond.

As you read about your response pattern, you'll discover many sources of strength. You'll also see that if your strengths go too far, they can become your weaknesses. This

DISC FOR DINNER

TYPICAL D, I, S, AND C RESPONSES TO FOOD:

D
- SOMETIMES EATS OVER THE SINK
- LIKES TO TRY NEW, EXOTIC FOODS
- LOVES TO MICROWAVE EVERYTHING, EVEN WATER
- NEVER FOLLOWS RECIPES
- EATS OUT A LOT

I
- ENTERTAINS A GREAT DEAL
- LIKES GOURMET FOODS
- HAS THE LATEST KITCHEN GADGETS, BUT DOESN'T USE THEM
- IS ATTRACTED TO FANCY PACKAGING
- WANTS TO KNOW WHAT FRIENDS ARE COOKING FOR DINNER

S
- VALUES MEALS AND CONSIDERS THEM IMPORTANT FAMILY TIME
- CONSIDERS THE KITCHEN THE MOST IMPORTANT ROOM IN THE HOUSE
- FOLLOWS THE USDA'S FOOD PYRAMID
- LIKES TO EXCHANGE RECIPES
- COOKS WHATEVER ANYONE WANTS TO EAT, EVEN IF THAT MEANS EATING THINGS HE OR SHE DOESN'T LIKE

C
- READS THE LABELS
- KNOWS THE PERCENTAGES OF PROTEIN, FAT, AND CARBOHYDRATES IN FOODS
- SHOPS FOR GOOD PRICES AND USES COUPONS
- BUYS KITCHEN GADGETS IF THEY ARE ECONOMICAL AND WELL-CONSTRUCTED
- TAKES A FAT OR CALORIE GUIDEBOOK TO A RESTAURANT

is true for all the responses: D, I, S, C. Too much of a good thing isn't so good anymore. The negative sides of our responses usually come out when we're under pressure. In your profile, you'll see options to consider if you see this happening to you.

As you read about your pattern, circle statements that seem particularly accurate for you in this situation, and cross out things that don't fit. Read your feedback and consider it carefully. Make use of the information you find helpful, and disregard the information that is not.

The Dominance Style: Direct and Decisive

D MOTTOS

- **TELL IT LIKE IT IS.**
- **WE SHALL OVERCOME.**
- **JUST DO IT.**

A high-D response to a situation shows that you are being strong-willed and strong-minded.

You are being decisive about your goals, and you are not afraid of conflict or of people objecting to your ideas. Nor are you shying away from obstacles as you work toward your goals. To other people, you might seem stubborn or headstrong, but that's okay with you. In this situation, you don't want to give in to the objections of others, or even to be told what to do. If there are rules to be made, you want to make them.

You are goal oriented. You believe that risks can be acceptable. Although you set high standards for yourself and enjoy the challenge of meeting them, you may have little patience, especially with those who seem to slow progress toward the goal. You are willing to persevere and see things through to the end if you have evidence of real progress.

You speak your mind, even if what you have to say is negative. However, you aren't an idle complainer; if you don't think that speaking out will change an unhappy situation for the better, you will hold your peace. Nevertheless, some people may find you blunt, even curt. You probably have little patience for these people, and you are even proud of your ability and willingness to speak directly and honestly, regardless of the reactions of others.

Along with your directness of approach comes a drive to act decisively. In this situation, it is important to you to get things moving quickly and to keep them moving.

You want to compete and win.

D: HOW YOU SEE THE SITUATION

Favorable	**You have power or control.**
Unfavorable	You lack power or control.

Value to the Group

A lot of organizations prize and reward people who come across as strong-willed, strong-minded, decisive, and dominant. In fact, many organizations and many people focus narrowly on the D style as *the* winning approach to business (though in reality, organizations need people of all styles).

In this situation, you are the initiator of action. Not only are you not afraid of risks, but you thrive on them.

Dominance Style

What motivates you?

➢ Control over your work environment
➢ Directing other people's activities
➢ New opportunities and challenges
➢ Opportunities for advancement

What discourages you?

➢ Being questioned or overruled
➢ Limited responsibility for results
➢ Restricted access to resources
➢ Close supervision

What is your favorite environment?

➢ Maximum freedom to determine how things are done
➢ Fast-paced
➢ Results-oriented

What do you avoid?

➢ Appearing soft or weak
➢ Routine, predictable situations
➢ Being micromanaged

Most important, you are able to identify the changes that will make the situation better.

You are often content to work alone; however, whether you do the work yourself, work with others, or assign tasks to others, your aim is to accomplish the task quickly. You like to streamline the process, make it efficient. You cut to the bottom line.

Areas of Misunderstanding

Your straight-ahead style may lead some people to think that you are self-centered or uncaring. Well, be honest—do you pause to help others or to ask their opinion of what you are doing? Often the support of others isn't that important to you. This, combined with your decisiveness, can create the impression that you care only about yourself.

Usually you don't allow yourself to move ahead without thinking about consequences, but—and this is important—you may be *perceived* as somebody who does just that.

Since you don't need a lot of encouragement or praise, you may not realize that these things are very important to some people.

Information to Share

Here are some things you might choose to share with others:

- You like work direction to be given in an open, friendly manner rather than by direct command.
- You are at your best when you can work on your own.
- You are not comfortable having to depend on other people.

- You enjoy moving quickly on ideas that appeal to you.
- You appreciate it when others support your ideas.
- You appreciate it when others allow you room to experiment.
- You tend to be impatient with people who can't decide or don't act quickly enough for you.

Now, should you present your co-workers with the above list, then tell them: "Hey, this is me. Take it or leave it"? Of course not. The idea is to *share information,* not offend others by presenting a list of demands.

Let's say your boss approaches you one morning with an assignment: "I need you to come up with some ideas for spreading the word about our new product. Maybe you can work with Bill and Mary on it."

You have a high-D response: You want to take charge of this project and run with it—alone. You might say to your boss, "That's exciting. Would it be all right with you if I put together a few ideas on my own before bringing Bill and Mary in on the project?"

Suggesting in this way that you work alone is an effective but nonoffensive way to share your insights into what your D style means.

Let's say that you find yourself part of a team assigned to produce a report. You are aware that you think and write quickly but that you have little patience with studying data at the start of the process and then reviewing, revising, editing, and proofreading the report at the end of the process. Let the other members of the team in on a few secrets: "People, my strength is drafting the report. I can really nail it—once I'm given the research. Then, after I draft the report, it would be very helpful if one of you would go over it, clean it up, and check it out."

Inviting Input

Some statements will shut down a discussion, cutting you off from important information and points of view. Choose words that invite others to share what they know. The keys are building on what others say and asking questions to keep the door open.

Instead of saying: "I like your plan, but you've forgotten something important."

Try: "I like your plan. Could we consider adding a section on _____?"

Instead of saying: "That's not the way I see it."

Try: "You may find it interesting to hear about my experience and how it's different from yours. Then will you tell me about your experience?"

Instead of saying: "That's an interesting idea, BUT it's never going to fly.

Try: "That's an interesting idea AND here is another thought."

What to Look Out For

It's easy to get swept away by your own D-ness. Try to keep in mind that in the situation you have focused on, you may be more self-reliant than others would be. This could mislead you into assuming that others don't need help, advice, or guidance. On the other hand, others may think you need help, which you'll find annoying.

Maybe it seems to you that there are no limits to what you can accomplish. Under the best conditions, such energy and self-confidence are contagious; however, others may not share your optimism, enthusiasm, confidence, or get-up-and-go. You won't want their advice that you should ease up, move more cautiously, or even take a break. No wonder, since your drive has probably been well rewarded in the past. However, be aware that, in your determination to get the job done, you may neglect to seek or to accept the input of those around you. You may be tempted to pass up valuable opportunities to acquire additional perspectives on a project or a problem and even opportunities to build support for your plan.

Getting Unstuck

Situation: When you speak your mind, people look stunned or upset.

Possibility: Before offering a comment or criticism, ask for permission. Say, "Do you want my thoughts on this project?" or, "Do you have the time now to discuss this project?"

Situation: You aren't being given enough chances to work alone.

Possibility: Your self-guided projects will go over better if you take the time to explain what you are doing. People showing some DiSC styles crave more background information than others, but just about everyone likes being kept in the loop.

Situation: You're having trouble getting acceptance for your plan.

Possibility: You like to cut to the bottom line, but some others need to know how you got there. Instead of just announcing your conclusions, take them through your process.

Situation: The final results aren't what you'd hoped for.

Possibility: In your drive to reach the goal, you may have overlooked some details. Slow down and take the time to think through all the consequences.

Situation: When others talk, you tune out.

Possibility: If you're missing critical information, you can sustain your attention by "active listening." Techniques include asking pointed questions and summing up the discussion from time to time.

Situation: Small talk drives you nuts.

Possibility: Your staff wants to start the weekly status meeting with ten minutes of socializing. Try mentally—or even formally—scheduling ten minutes for this purpose. Then you won't feel that you're getting behind schedule.

Situation: Someone who works for you has developed a "bad attitude."

Possibility: You don't need a lot of feedback, so you may not realize how much some people crave it. Does the person need regular performance reviews, public recognition, or even just the occasional praise for good work?

Your Bottom Line

In this focus situation, your direct, forceful manner can inspire others when they recognize the value of your insights and contributions. Be careful that your drive to go your own way doesn't alienate or worry others. Your willingness to experiment and take risks can be valuable

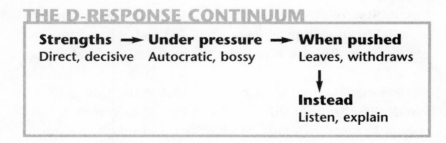

THE D-RESPONSE CONTINUUM

Strengths ➞ **Under pressure** ➞ **When pushed**
Direct, decisive   Autocratic, bossy   Leaves, withdraws

⬇

Instead
Listen, explain

to the group, especially if you decide to invest time and effort in building support for your plan.

This Style in Action

People who consistently show a high-D style can both energize and exhaust a group, creating inspiration as well as intimidation. The high-D style is especially well suited to the corporate champion, the individual who pushes a key project to completion, against all odds.

For example, Bill had been designing custom software since the earliest days of the personal computer. Over the years, he developed a specialty of creating programs to solve the complex problems of "just-in-time" inventory management. He helped companies minimize costs by ordering goods only as they are needed, without jeopardizing production schedules.

A few years ago, a major manufacturer of small appliances asked Bill to design a "just-in-time" program to a long list of stringent specifications. Bill knew that this one was going to be tough and that other people, including his boss, had no idea just how tough. Accordingly, when he set to work on the project, he carefully sheltered it from potential internal critics, from his boss, and even from the client. He looked at the issued specifications and decided that they wouldn't work out. He laid them aside and concentrated instead on developing concepts that his own experience and experiments indicated would work.

Ultimately, he designed about 85 percent of the product on his own. Working within—as well as around—his own firm, he called on help from others informally and unofficially. Once he developed an alpha version of the software for this client, it failed—thirteen times!

Now the deadline for a beta version was closing in.

"When will we see something, Bill?" his boss started asking.

"I'm just about there," Bill would answer.

He was confident he was. He saw those thirteen failed alphas not as disasters, but as learning experiences. From them, putting them together and taking them apart, he delivered a virtually bug-free beta version right on schedule. It didn't meet the client's specs—it exceeded them. Bill had given the client more than the client had asked for, solving problems the client's specs had failed to address.

The Influence Style: Optimistic and Outgoing

CHAPTER FIVE

- **IT'S NOT WHAT YOU KNOW, IT'S WHO YOU KNOW.**
- **PEOPLE ARE MORE IMPORTANT THAN THINGS.**
- **LET'S BOOGIE.**

If you responded to the situation with high I, you are being a "people person." You are finding it rewarding to be with other people, and they're enjoying you, too. Being a "people person" can take many forms. Perhaps you make friends easily. Perhaps you network. You love meetings, socializing, schmoozing, recognition ceremonies.

Enthusiastic and cheerful, you are being both expressive and demonstrative. Other people might call you outgoing, open, or extroverted. You are eager to share your ideas, and you communicate in a lively way. You attract and are attracted to other people, and you are in your element when you're part of a team. Under the right circumstances, your positive energy is contagious.

Favorable	You have power or control.
Unfavorable	You lack power or control.

Value to the Group

An I response helps pull together groups of people, forges teams, and gets diverse people to cooperate.

If you are responding with high I, you may find yourself chosen as a spokesperson. When others have a new idea or project to promote, they'll want you on their side. When a new idea or project is introduced, you may well be the person who delivers the message.

High-I, business-oriented small talk is valuable to the group, too. A little light conversation in the hall or at the coffee machine can lift morale and build a sense of team.

Areas of Misunderstanding

Your friendly manner is an open invitation to others. In this situation, other people may confide in you and ask for your help. The trouble is, they may think you have inexhaustible stores of patience and empathy. The gap between perception and reality may lead some people to think you're insensitive or even phony.

Information to Share

While you are good at influencing other people, you don't feel responsible for them. It's not that you don't care about other people, it's that your approach is so warm, friendly,

Influence Style

What motivates you?

➤ Dialoguing with others

➤ Immediate verbal feedback

➤ Enthusiastic recognition

➤ Acknowledgment of your feelings

What discourages you?

➤ Reserved or unfriendly co-workers

➤ Rigid schedules

➤ Pessimism

➤ Routine, detailed tasks

What is your favorite environment?

➤ Fast-paced

➤ Positive feedback and recognition

➤ Lots of variety and creativity

What do you avoid?

➤ Conflict

➤ Losing approval

➤ Detailed tasks

➤ Repetitive tasks

➤ Working alone

open, and compelling that it may create unrealistic expectations. Talking to you, a person may feel that he or she has instantly made a best friend—whether that is the message you wanted to deliver or not.

Since you are outgoing and expressive, however, you should find it relatively easy to share this and other key information about yourself.

If you tend to be a high I in groups, be prepared to volunteer for the following people-oriented tasks:

- recruiting others
- persuading others
- building confidence in others
- building teams

It is certainly possible for you to work alone, but your I-driven inclination is for group efforts, especially when there's a need to muster and marshal forces.

What to Look Out For

People who respond with a high-I dimension have trouble following through on tasks. In this situation, you may well be great at getting things started but have trouble following through with all the details—until you're willing to discipline yourself.

Also, among some groups and at some times and places, sociability can become a liability. This is especially true in situations calling for quiet, solitary work. It is not so much that you will disturb others as that you may put off such solo activities as research, study, or writing. You are not lazy or prone to procrastination, but you bloom in a group, and you don't feel very comfortable when you are working alone.

Getting Unstuck
Situation: Little details keep tripping up your project.
Possibilities: All those picky details are boring to you, but they can derail the whole train. Try disciplining yourself to pay attention to the small stuff. Or partner up with someone who loves the details.

Situation: You think the glass is always half full.
Possibility: Are you seeing people and situations for what they really are? Open yourself up to see their negative sides. It's great to be a positive force, but you need to be realistic, or things won't work out well in the end.

Situation: You want to chat, but the other person acts cold.
Possibility: Some people don't like to schmooze the way you do. Look for people who like to shoot the breeze as much as you do.

Situation: You see it as schmoozing, your boss sees it as a waste of time.
Possibility: Point out that time spent building business relationships can pay off big time.

Your Bottom Line
Day in and day out, organizations need "people persons" like you.

In your focus situation, you probably tend to conform rather than go your own way. It's not that you are a follower, not a leader, but that you are more comfortable with consensus than with conflict. You don't just give in to others, but you do adjust to them and to their needs. This will earn you respect and affection.

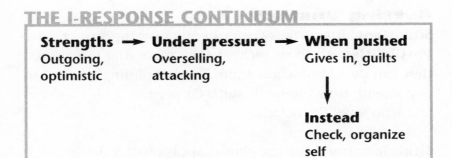

Strengths ➤ **Under pressure** ➤ **When pushed**
Outgoing,   Overselling,   Gives in, guilts
optimistic   attacking

                                                                    ↓

                                                            Instead
                                                            Check, organize
                                                            self

This Style in Action

"So you put in the new customer database software at your place?"

"We did," Ed Perkins replied, stabbing another hors d'oeuvre with a toothpick. "And I'm amazed at just how smoothly it went. The people in our office got onto it in a snap. I mean, *everybody* is just so used to working with computers now. It's like second nature."

"It sure wasn't always like that."

"No," Ed nodded, "indeed, it wasn't. I remember when we introduced the first generation of the database software. Boy, we were scared. The boss—you know Jane Campbell, right?—was worried about a steep learning curve, losing productivity, even losing employees. See, she was especially concerned that the staff would actively *resist* learning the new software. You know, these people had been doing the job for a long time, doing it *their* way, and doing it pretty darn good. So here we were, about to tell them, 'No. Now you've got to do it this way, and you've got to learn a whole new process.'

"Well, Jane and I were talking about how we were going to introduce the new system, and as we were talking, I happened to look down the hall. There were about half a dozen people gathered around Tom Peterson. You remember Tom?"

"Who *doesn't* remember Tom?"

"That's right. Warm, friendly, great salesman. Not **too** eager to tackle the market research stats, though. And, I have to say, once, when we assigned him to proofread the ad copy for a new product line—well, let's just say a *lot* of i's were left undotted and t's uncrossed. But, with people, **one** on-one-and especially in a group, he's always been extremely effective. You just can't help listening to him.

"So, anyway, I was watching this crowd around Tom, hanging on his every word, and a lightbulb went on in my head, and I just suddenly said to Jane, 'Let's get Tom to do it.'

"She says, 'What. . .?'

"I tell her, 'Tom is a natural-born salesman, a persuader, a closer. Instead of going directly to the staff with a tech manual or a trainer, let's do it through Tom. Let's pull him in on the new database right now, get him up to speed, then turn him loose on the staff.'

"I don't mind telling you that Jane didn't exactly leap at the idea. 'He's not a techie, you know,' she said. 'I don't think he even *likes* computers.'

"'That doesn't matter,' I said. 'People like *him*. They listen to him. They are persuaded by him. If we get Tom on board, the others will follow. It may take some work to get him up to speed on this project, but if we explain what we want him to do and why we want him to do it, he'll do it—even if he *hates* computers. For him, the computers aren't the issue. It's the people.'"

"So how did it turn out?"

"Well, I do have to admit that getting Tom up to speed on the software was something of a major chore. But he stuck with it. He was frustrated at times, but he stuck with it, learned it, and then just went out among the folks like a tiger.

"Of course, we didn't expect him to do a full-scale technical training seminar. We just wanted him to break the ice, provide an overview, and, most of all, to communicate just why it was important to convert to the new system and why it was important for everyone to become super-proficient with it. Once Tom had overcome the resistance out there, we brought in the techies with their demo programs, overhead projectors, and the most tedious hour and a half of videos I've ever sat through. But the people all stuck with it, and the learning curve wasn't all that steep. We were up and running much faster than I thought we'd be."

The Supportiveness Style: Sympathetic and Cooperative

CHAPTER SIX

S MOTTOS

- DON'T ROCK THE BOAT.
- A BIRD IN THE HAND IS WORTH TWO IN THE BUSH.
- LIKE A ROCK.
- I'LL BE THERE.

When you have a high-S response to a situation, you are showing that you are ready, able, and willing to help others. You want to make things easier for everyone. You don't wait to be asked—you *look* for ways to be helpful. In addition, your actions are usually guided by a strong wish to be reasonable and fair.

You don't like conflict, and you even let others have their own way rather than start an argument. You look for solutions that are acceptable to everybody. You don't always cave in, but often what others want is just fine with you, as long as it won't cause sudden, radical change. You like stability, though you will support a change as long as you understand why it's necessary.

Favorable	You have power or control.
Unfavorable	You lack power or control.

Value to the Group

What work group wouldn't value a person who loves to help out?

You also help bring out the best in others. You offer praise and encouragement, and when constructive criticism is needed, your tact and good humor make it go down easy (you'll help find solutions to the problem, too).

Areas of Misunderstanding

Helpful and supportive, you are easy to get along with. Usually that's great for everyone, but some people may think you don't want to take part when decisions are made. In fact, if there are problems to be solved, you want to be part of the process.

Because you don't complain much, your co-workers may not realize how much you're troubled by sudden or constant change.

Your conservatism in this situation can be valuable to the group. If you move cautiously, it's because you tend to see the risks that come along with change. Other people may not have seen these risks, and you can help the group by pointing out the potential problems. However, some in the group may misread your caution as stubbornness, a lack of imagination, or a lack of ambition. It's great to be the voice of caution—just be aware that some people find the voice of caution annoying.

Supportiveness Style

What motivates you?

➤ Cooperating with others

➤ Clearly defined responsibility and authority

➤ Providing good service

➤ Job security

What discourages you?

➤ Rapid, unpredictable change

➤ Competitiveness

➤ Aggressiveness

➤ Lack of support from managers or co-workers

➤ Confrontation

What is your favorite environment?

➤ Predictable and orderly

➤ Harmonious

➤ Informal

➤ Friendly

What do you avoid?

➤ Unpredictable or uncertain situations

➤ Disorganized and disorderly workplaces

Information to Share

Let others know that you are happiest and most effective at work when you are fully informed about the task at hand and the reasons for doing things in a certain way.

It is important to try to speak up for yourself. You are flexible, but you don't want to go along with anything and everything others want. If you don't ask the questions that are in your mind, others may take your compliance for granted, and they will be unpleasantly surprised, disappointed, perhaps even angry when you don't fall in line.

Since you enjoy working behind the scenes, you might volunteer for tasks that won't put you out front. Just don't let yourself be buried, ignored, and generally taken for granted.

What to Look Out For

Because you do not want to be the focus of attention or the cause of problems, you're inclined to keep your feelings to yourself. This approach produces one result you like: People like your easygoing nature. But you run the risk of being taken for granted, and you may not be consulted when changes are proposed. This is not only potentially damaging to your career, but it makes you unhappy. If change must occur, you want to be informed, and you want to have input into the decisions that are made. Also, it's hard to go through day after day without talking about the things that bother you.

Getting Unstuck

Situation: Your routine is being disrupted.
Possibility: Take small steps toward becoming more flexible about routines and changes. Becoming flexible about

change is like becoming flexible at the health club; the more often you stretch, the easier it gets.

Situation: You're upset over a big change.
Possibility: You'll feel more comfortable if you have complete information, so ask lots of questions. Wording your questions positively will encourage the other person to respond openly, frankly, and fully. Instead of asking, "Why do we have to change?" try "That sounds exciting. How do you think the new plan will make things better?"

Situation: You rarely speak up in meetings.
Possibilities: Tell people, one-on-one, that you tend to be a bit reserved, but you appreciate being asked your opinion. Practice by speaking out on smaller issues and ones that aren't surrounded by heated emotions. What you have to say is valuable, so speak up.

Situation: When someone praises you, you brush it off.
Possibility: Many people who respond with a high S are overly modest. Next time, take the compliment. Instead of making little of your accomplishment, just look the person in the eye and say a simple "thank you." Then focus for thirty seconds on letting it in.

Your Bottom Line

Your modesty is charming and disarming, but it is not always good to play down your many contributions. Even if you do play down your role, don't be surprised if other people are quick to appreciate your supportiveness and bring you their concerns. They know that you will listen and that you will hold their comments in confidence. That's good.

You may not be eager to volunteer your keen insights into current situations. If asked, you will almost certainly oblige by sharing your thoughts, but if you are not asked, you may keep silent.

You are patient, supportive, and steady. For better or worse, you may not be seen as working on the cutting edge. However, people know they can depend on you.

THE S-RESPONSE CONTINUUM

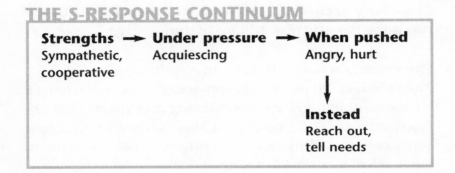

Strengths ➞ **Under pressure** ➞ **When pushed**
Sympathetic,   Acquiescing   Angry, hurt
cooperative

                                         ↓

                                         Instead
                                         Reach out,
                                         tell needs

This Style in Action

Not long ago, many manufacturing companies sharply divided their operations in two: front office and back office. Front-office staff included the salespeople, who went out and got the business, while back-office staff were support personnel, including customer service. The front-office people got all the glory. Customer service was the *last* place a career-minded individual wanted to be.

Today, this has changed, especially where the product is complex or technical. High-tech businesses have discovered that customers put a high premium on the human service behind the technology. PC suppliers all offer similar technology, so the point of difference becomes customer service.

High-tech firms call their customer-service operations "customer support." Support—that comes natural to anyone who takes a high-S approach. Here's how this can look.

Jane picked up the telephone and was blasted by the panicky voice of a branch manager for a major investment firm. Something was terribly wrong. Somehow, someone (Jane suspected it was the branch manager himself, but said nothing) had improperly set the password coding for the PCs on their network. Every time they tried to execute a customer transaction, they ran into a software roadblock.

"Do something. *Anything.* Now!"

Jane wanted to help. She always looked for opportunities to make life easier for her clients.

Jane also knew that she had to protect the security of the investment firm, as well as that of her own company. She knew that a quick fix that violated the security protocol would be no real help at all. In stressful situations like this, when time is critical and the customer needs immediate action, it takes thought to remember why the safety rules are there.

Jane explained, calmly and fully, why it was in the client's best interest for her to maintain the security protocol, even if it meant several more minutes of down time. She apologized for needing to check for a security breach, explaining that maintaining their internal security created a tough shield for them and for their customers. She did not resort to telling the branch manager that she was "following company policy," but rather explained the value of security protocol.

Jane recognized that she was working with a frustrated person. She expressed empathy and even apologized for the current circumstance. Next, she carefully explained the disasters that could occur if the firm's computers had been breached and everyone was being duped into helping the hackers. Then she offered reassurance, making sure that the person on the other end of the phone did not feel *he* was being accused.

After the crisis had been resolved, Jane remarked to the customer that the entire experience had demonstrated the security value that the investment firm could promote to its customers.

She had turned panic into relief, and a near disaster into an episode of customer satisfaction.

The Consciousness Style: Concerned and Correct

CHAPTER SEVEN

C MOTTOS

- A STITCH IN TIME SAVES NINE.
- GET YOUR DUCKS IN A ROW.
- IT'S ALL IN THE DETAILS.
- DO IT RIGHT THE FIRST TIME.

In this situation, you are concerned with doing things well. You are a stickler for quality. You spend time thinking carefully about tasks assigned to you or tasks you undertake on your own initiative. You are less interested in getting a job done quickly than you are in doing it right.

You hold others to high standards, but you are even more demanding of yourself. Indeed, you find it very satisfying to set your bar high, then go even higher. When you occasionally fall short of your own mark, you may feel very disappointed in yourself.

Value to the Group

The group turns to someone having a high-C response

67

Conscientiousness Style

What motivates you?

➤ Wanting to be right

➤ Logical, systematic approaches

➤ Rewards for quality and accuracy

➤ Specific feedback

What discourages you?

➤ Rules or expectations that change constantly without explanation

➤ Lack of time to process information

➤ Mandatory socializing

➤ Lack of quality controls

What is your favorite environment?

➤ The time and resources to perform to your own standards

➤ Reserved, businesslike, and task-oriented

What do you avoid?

➤ Being criticized

➤ Lack of time to evaluate consequences

➤ Emotionally charged situations

➤ Disclosing personal information

C: HOW YOU SEE THE SITUATION

Favorable	You have power or control.
Unfavorable	**You lack power or control.**

when something has to be done absolutely right. If you have a reputation for producing high-quality results, you may be called on to evaluate and inspect the work of others, including products and services from outside suppliers.

In this situation, you are following rules and guidelines, but if they start to interfere with your ability to produce a high-quality result, you may complain or reluctantly work to change them.

Your insistence on careful planning may make demands on the group but is valuable to it. Thanks to you, projects go forward only after thorough preparation and consideration.

Areas of Misunderstanding

Some people will find your high standards intimidating. They think that you are continually judging them and that they can never measure up. Some will resent having the bar set so high. While some people will be grateful when you check their work, others will find this annoying, picky, or threatening.

In this situation, you probably have strong ideas about how to minimize mistakes. If you insist that others follow your procedures, you may come across as controlling. Actually, you are not interested in controlling anyone—it's not personal—you just want to produce a high-quality result.

Information to Share

Let others know that you want a clear understanding of a

task before you begin. You are particularly interested in knowing their expectations of you. Emphasize that thorough communication and clear instructions are important to you. Incomplete or fuzzy directions make you uncomfortable. If you feel you don't have enough information, you may try to cover all contingencies. Those who do not understand your reasons may say you are creating backups for your backup.

Find out just what is required and expected. Also, make your standards and expectations clear—not only what you expect of your own work, but also what you expect of others. Create ground rules, standards, and checklists. Decide how you can meet the standards, expectations, and requirements of the group without sacrificing quality or your own standards.

If others accuse you of being overly critical, it may help to clarify that when you evaluate their work, you are, indeed, evaluating their work, not them as human beings.

What to Look Out For

It may be hard for you to accept that perfection isn't always possible, necessary, or even desirable. Important opportunities may be lost by waiting for perfection; sometimes a good solution *now* is better than a perfect solution *later.*

Getting Unstuck

Situation: Another deadline was missed.
Possibility: When possible, set your own deadlines a few days short, so you have time to go back over everything without missing the real deadline.

Situation: Your manager is angry because the report is taking so long.
Possibility: Watch out for situations in which "good enough" really is good enough. You might ask the manager

why it is important to act now. Perhaps he or she knows something you don't.

Situation: You don't like it when other people find an error in your work.
Possibility: Consider that they may only be trying to help. Perhaps they've thought of something that's escaped your attention and that can improve the quality of the outcome.

Situation: You're burning out.
Possibility: Try to loosen up a bit. No one has to be right all the time.

Situation: Your constructive criticism is resented.
Possibilities: Your willingness to offer constructive criticism is valuable, but it's good to balance this by offering praise from time to time. You don't have to be phony about it. The next time you examine someone's work, look for something to compliment. If you find it, tell the person.

Your Bottom Line

It's great that you produce quality on your own and that you help ensure that others also produce quality. Just be aware that some people may find your commitment to excellence intimidating. While remaining open to the needs and feelings of others, make it clear that your passion for high standards is focused on the job at hand, not on the personalities of your colleagues, co-workers, subordinates, or bosses.

This Style in Action

High quality satisfies customers, bosses, investors, colleagues, subordinates, and you.

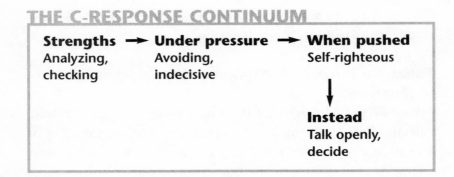

Strengths → **Under pressure** → **When pushed**

Analyzing,   Avoiding,   Self-righteous

checking   indecisive

↓

Instead

Talk openly,

decide

People who often use a C-style behavior pattern enjoy a special opportunity to create quality. In his 1994 book, *Leading Your Positively Outrageous Service Team*, customer service consultant T. Scott Gross shares a General Motors ad that impressed him. This was its headline: "We blew a deadline, ticked everyone off, cost the company a bundle, and we did the right thing."

Then the ad continued:

What if you ran a division of General Motors and were due to debut an important flagship model . . . and it wasn't quite ready yet? Nothing drastic, you understand, just a few glitches that meant that not every car coming off the line was just right. What if you'd sworn to your bosses that you'd be ready? What if you had a lot of potential customers waiting to get a first look? What would you do? Here's what Jim Perkins and his team did: They pulled the plug on the introduction and said, "When we know we've got it right, we'll bring out the car." That night, Jim Perkins did what people who do the right thing always do. He got a good night's sleep.

The implication is unmistakable: A commitment to doing the right thing the right way is a winning strategy for everyone involved.

People-Reading

The objective of people-reading is to enable you to communicate and collaborate with others by connecting with points of view beyond your own. This can lead to more productive and more satisfying working relationships.

So far, we've focused on *your* thoughts, feelings, and behavior in a specific situation that is important to you. But you probably aren't the only person involved in the situation. One person, or many other people, are having their own thoughts and feelings about the situation, and they are behaving in ways that you may like a lot, or not like at all.

Every one of these people has a point of view on this situation. Some people will look at it in ways similar to how you do, and some people will look at it in ways so radically different that you might wonder if they should have their vision checked. No, they see just fine; it's just that they are wearing different glasses than you are.

Picture this. Four people look at the same situation. One looks through bright red glasses and has a high-D response. The second, looking through spangled silver frames, has a high-I response. The third, looking through warm yellow frames, has a high-S response. The fourth, looking through black-and-white checked frames, has a high-C response. Each sees the situation differently.

What kind of glasses are the other people in your situation wearing?

And, just as important, are your glasses different from theirs?

Nothing Personal

If you put a bright blue patch and a bright red patch side by side, the colors clash. They may even seem to vibrate. The colors do not choose to do this, nor do our eyes and brains choose to see the great contrast. It just happens: a phenomenon of physics and perception.

Put a D-responding person and an S-responding person together, and the result may also be a clash. The two people don't choose to clash. It just happens. If you can accept this, it'll be easier to step back from a situation and see it more calmly. The difficult person isn't trying to ruin your day.

Many times, what people call a "conflict of personalities" is a misunderstanding of the other person's perspective. Such clashes can *seem* purposeful and personal when, in reality, they are the unconscious or unintentional results of the collision of styles.

For example, Jane may think that John is a jerk who is deliberately causing trouble for her, but his behavior may be driven by a point of view that's just different from Jane's. John may be guided by a high-C outlook, while Jane sees things in a D way. John didn't choose his high-C point of view any more than Jane chose her strongly D perspective. Also, John's C orientation has nothing to do with Jane's D inclinations. If a conflict results from the collision of these two points of view, there is nothing personal about it.

Real Jerks versus Situational Jerks

Some conflicts do get personal. After taking DiSC in a workshop, someone asked, "Is there a fifth style you didn't mention? Someone we know uses the 'O' style—'O' for obnoxious. Instead of DiSC, why not DiSCO?"

It's true that there are people who are selfish, manipulative, or downright mean. However, there's a difference between a "genetic jerk" and a "situational jerk." A genetic jerk will never change, no matter what anyone does or says. If the person is a situational jerk, though, there's hope. Most jerks we encounter are situational jerks. They are acting that way because of the situation they're in.

If you use DiSC to reflect on why the person is being a jerk, you're already starting to give him or her the benefit of the doubt. Instead of judging the person, you're trying to understand what's going on.

Sharing DiSC

The best way to find out someone else's response style is to ask him or her to take the tool and to share the results. If you're excited about what you're learning, pass it on!

Ideally, everybody you work with would take DiSC and use the results. In many organizations, DiSC workshops have fostered understanding, cooperation, acceptance, and trust—the keys to top performance in today's increasingly diverse and team-oriented workplace. Perhaps the greatest benefit is a common language for talking about feelings, thoughts, and behavior. This language is objective and non-judgmental. It describes what is, not what should be. DiSC can help your group communicate better and focus on issues, rather than on "personality conflicts."

If you'd like to go about this with some professional guidance, you can contact Inscape for a list of authorized facilitators in your area.

For you as an individual, though, it's probably not a good idea to play trainer if you have no experience. We recommend that you spread the word about DiSC one person at a time. Do what comes natural. If you've worked with someone for a while, and you think he or she would be open to this self-learning, tell that person about this book and about DiSC.

You tell a friend, and that person tells a friend . . . .

Adults are just-in-time learners. When they need to learn something, they learn it then. That's why it's true, as the saying goes, that when the student is ready, the teacher will appear. If you try to interest someone who just isn't ready, you'll just frustrate yourself. On the other hand, if you're mentoring someone, it might be entirely appropriate to suggest this tool.

It would be great if all of the people involved in a situation ran to their desks, took DiSC, and shared their results and new insights. But you live in the real world. So you need a way to make an educated guess of the other person's likely response. That's where people-reading comes in.

Reading Others

People aren't cartoon characters with little thought bubbles revealing how they're responding to the situation, so how can you tell who's exhibiting D, I, S, or C behavior?

First, draw on your intuition. By now, you have a feel for the four dimensions. It's very likely that you've already started to spot DiSC dimensions in other people's responses. Many people say they can't stop themselves from using DiSC this way.

You can hone your DiSC intuition by rereading chapters 4 through 7, which describe the four single response patterns.

Keep in mind the very important difference between looking at your response to a situation and looking at someone else's response. When you use the DiSC instrument, you look at your feelings and thoughts and behaviors. When you look at other people, you can see only behaviors, because it's impossible to go inside someone else's head and know what he or she is thinking and feeling. Instead of making assumptions, focus on the actions you can see.

Behaviors are good clues, though. Behaviors don't just happen; they are caused by the way people are feeling and thinking about a situation. So it is useful to become a skillful observer of the ways people act in a situation.

DiSC will help you be a better observer. It will also help you sort out what you observe so that you can make educated guesses about behavioral styles.

As always with DiSC, keep repeating the mantra "in this situation" while reflecting on behavior and while applying the results. People will show different styles in different situations. If you assume that others will always react the same way, you may become prejudiced about them. You can start pigeonholing people or limiting their responsibilities or careers. DiSC should help you interact and work with others more effectively and satisfyingly. It should not be used as an excuse to dismiss or short-sell others.

People-Reading Signs

Each response is characterized by the following *observable* qualities.

Dominance
- Decides quickly
- Takes action
- Moves quickly
- Takes charge
- Goes first
- Takes bold, often aggressive action
- Gets right to the point
- Tells others what to do
- Expresses concern for the bottom line

Influence
- Starts conversations easily and readily
- Fun to be with
- Expresses optimism
- Makes friends easily
- Generally outgoing
- Persuades others

Supportiveness
- Follows orders
- Avoids causing problems
- Avoids arguments
- Listens patiently
- Demonstrates understanding of others' feelings
- Relates to others warmly
- Rarely makes demands of others
- Easy to get along with
- "Nice person"

Conscientiousness
- Has a place for everything, everything in its place
- Is careful, perhaps guarded, when speaking
- Thinks things through
- Not impulsive
- Stickler for quality
- Detailed reports and memos
- Plans ahead
- Seems to want to work alone

While it can be helpful (and fun) to identify DiSC behavior dimensions in others, don't fall into the trap of labeling people with DiSC terminology. Remember, DiSC is dynamic, not static; it depends heavily on the situation. It is *not* a permanent designation of personality type. In a different situation the person may behave quite differently.

You won't be able to figure out a complex double or triple response pattern, just a single high dimension. But that may well be enough to help you make sense of the situation and get it unstuck.

Carrying the Bucket

Such people-reading can be the first step toward reducing "relationship tension" between yourself and another person.

When you work with someone, it's as if you're carrying a bucket. When you first meet the other person, your bucket is empty. Each time the other person does something that grates on you, water is added to the bucket. Water is heavy, and after a while you're carrying around a very heavy bucket. The relationship feels like a burden, and it weighs you down all day long. You probably feel resentment or anger; on top of everything else you have to get done, you have to carry around that bucket.

The heavier your bucket, the smaller the chance of a productive working relationship. You'll probably stop listening to what the other person is saying. You're too busy talking to yourself: "I can't wait to get out of here" or "I wish I could tell him what I really think of him." Relationship stress is like that.

Your bucket may hold a cup, or it may hold ten gallons—people have different capacities to absorb stress. At some point, though, everyone's bucket can fill to the top.

When your bucket is full and more is added, you will dump your bucket.

Each DiSC response is associated with certain ways of responding to mounting relationship stress and with certain styles of dumping the bucket.

A common D response to mounting relationship tension is to become bossy or autocratic. When D dumps the bucket, typical responses are to withdraw or walk away from the situation.

Typical I responses to mounting tension are overselling and attacking. When I dumps the bucket, common responses are giving in and laying guilt or blame on others.

Typical S responses to relationship tension are acquiescing and keeping quiet. The S way to dump is to become angry and hurt, but the feelings are kept inside.

Typical C behaviors under pressure are to avoid issues or to become indecisive. When C dumps the bucket, there are high emotions and self-righteousness.

These typical responses are understandable, but they are also damaging. They can make it difficult to repair the relationship.

There are alternatives to dumping the bucket. When you feel your bucket filling up, you can choose to do something instead of dump. You can lighten the bucket in a positive and productive way. The alternatives are:

- For D: Instead of withdrawing, listen and explain.
- For I: Instead of attacking, stop, step back, and get organized.
- For S: Instead of getting hurt and angry, reach out and tell the person what you need.
- For C: Instead of avoiding decisions, make decisions; instead of becoming self-righteous, talk openly.

The following sections list a variety of responses that tend to reduce relationship tension. First, there is a list of actions that would probably make the other person feel more comfortable, open, receptive, or cooperative. The other person will understand, respect, or value actions like these. The second list is equally important; it describes ways that the other person's behavior may make you feel. They form an early warning system for you. It can be useful to you to have a plan for coping with behaviors that you personally will find difficult.

The lists are suggestions—you will choose the actions and responses that are right in your situation, and right for you.

Working with D

In everyday situations, a person showing high-D behavior is generally perceived as a take-charge type. Under pressure, this person tends to become demanding and may storm out of the room.

People who are driven by a strong D dimension like others to be direct, straightforward, and results-oriented. In relating to a person showing D-dimension behavior, try the following:

- Communicate briefly and to the point.
- Avoid small talk and other attempts to break the ice.
- Stick to the topic.
- Do what you can to respect this person's need for autonomy.
- Clearly communicate rules and expectations.
- Whenever possible, let the person initiate actions.
- Demonstrate your own competence.
- Display independence.

As for yourself, be prepared to cope with the following kinds of responses from the high-D person:

- blunt talk
- demands
- lack of empathy
- little interest in social interaction

Working with I

Normally, a high-I dimension prompts a persuading and enthusiastic approach to others. Under pressure, these individuals may push to oversell themselves, their point of view, or their project. In extreme situations, the high-I person acts dejected and may even pout.

People who are having a strong I response generally like others to be friendly, to show emotion, and to recognize and acknowledge contributions and achievements. In relating to the I dimension, try the following:

- Be informal.
- Schmooze.
- Listen up.
- Write down instructions.
- Publicly recognize accomplishments.
- Use humor.

Be prepared for any or all of the followings needs and responses:

- hunger for the limelight
- overly optimistic
- overselling ideas, points of view, or projects—especially under pressure
- takes rejection (perceived or real) hard

Working with S

Under normal conditions, the S dimension prompts behavior that is supportive and friendly. Under pressure, however, those with a strong S dimension tend to give in easily rather than argue or "create a problem." When backed up against a wall, this person may act hurt or may lash out with accusations.

People with a high-Supportiveness dimension like others to be relaxed, agreeable, cooperative, and appreciative. Here are some approaches that are helpful in relating to the S dimension of behavior:

- Be logical and systematic in your approach.
- Provide a secure environment.
- Avoid unnecessary changes.
- When change is necessary, try to ease the person into it; don't push; don't rush.
- Share information; let the person know how things will be done.
- Express sincere appreciation.
- In giving praise, emphasize the person's contribution to the group or team.

Be prepared for the following:

- friendliness to colleagues and supervisors alike
- resistance to change
- difficulty prioritizing tasks; a tendency to become overwhelmed
- difficulty with deadline pressures

Working with C

On a routine day, the person with a strong C dimension is careful and quiet. When the pressure builds, however, he or she may find it increasingly difficult to make decisions—especially when instant decisions are called for. In extreme situations, under great pressure, this quiet person may become highly emotional and may verbally attack others.

Those who have a strong C response like others to keep socializing to a minimum, to furnish full details concerning assignments and projects, and to demonstrate an appreciation of accuracy—of doing things well and right. In relating to this dimension of behavior, try the following:

- Make expectations clear, down to the smallest detail.
- Establish deadlines as far in advance as possible.
- Avoid unleashing surprises.
- Demonstrate your dependability.
- Show loyalty.
- Be tactful in your remarks.
- Avoid displays of emotion.
- Rely on precedent as a guide in current activities.
- Be precise and focused.
- Express value of high standards.

Be prepared to address the following responses and characteristics:

- discomfort with lack of clarity
- resistance to information that is general or vague
- strong urge to check and double-check work
- independence; little need to affiliate with others

Not a Good Idea

People-reading can be a great tool to help you reduce relationship stress and make the workplace a happier, more productive place. Like all tools, however, this one has to be used properly and safely.

Remember, identifying DiSC dimensions is *not* a diagnosis of personality. The purpose of DiSC is not to pigeonhole people. Pigeonholing denies the human capacity for change and adaptation. You work with living, breathing, thinking people, not programmed robots.

Nor should people-reading be used as a tool for manipulation. Manipulation is not only objectionable on ethical grounds, but it is ineffective in the long run.

While people-reading skills are extremely useful for reducing relationship tension, it's not a good idea to use DiSC to choose the people you work with or socialize with. In a group, diversity of all kinds—whether it's ethnic, cultural, gender-related, or related to DiSC styles—typically offers more advantages than uniformity. Behavioral styles don't always and inevitably clash.

Frequently, sharply different styles produce synergy. For example, when a D-responding person and an S-responding person collaborate on a project, aspects of the D may well complement those of the S and vice versa. For example, a D response can keep the focus on results, while an S response helps smooth the way so the goal is achieved without high drama or conflict in the group. Mutual admiration and respect may develop.

In fact, having too many people with the same responses doing the same kind of work is dangerous for a company. An organization needs to respond to its challenges in a whole range of ways. Also, innovations often come from people who might think they're in the wrong jobs. For example, someone who hates repetition might create shortcuts that help the whole organization.

The next chapter explores in greater depth your options for acting on the insights of DiSC in general and people-reading in particular.

You Choose

DiSC is a *tool*, not a *test*. The lists in the last chapter were a people-reading *tool*, not people-reading *rules*. Tests and rules tell people what to do, but with DiSC, you decide what to do. DiSC is your tool or instrument for gathering information. You decide how to act on this information. This chapter will help you make these decisions.

After you have taken the DiSC instrument, you have four options:

1. Do nothing.
2. Take action within your preferred style of behavior.
3. Adapt and act a different way.
4. Engage in a dialogue to find solutions.

Each route would demand more from you than the one before it, but each also offers greater potential rewards. In fact, resolving a situation may not be possible without going to the deeper level. On the other hand, sometimes the best action is no action at all.

Start by considering option 1, and work down the list until you reach the action that seems best for this particular situation, and for you.

Option 1: Do Nothing

Ask yourself three questions:

1. Is this situation important to me?
2. Is it possible to change this situation?
3. If it is possible to change this situation, is it worth the effort and risk involved?

Not everything needs to be fixed, including some things that are broken. Your world is busy. You may need to spend your time on other things. Other relationships or goals may need your attention more. You may need to save your energy, resources, or political capital for other battles.

So the first step is to ask, Is this situation important to me? If the answer is no, then say to yourself, FIDO: Forget It. Drive On! Save your attention for situations that matter to you.

Choosing to do nothing is a conscious action, and it is not the same as simply ignoring a situation.

Do you tend to avoid conflicts as much as possible? The question is not whether the situation makes you uncomfortable, but whether it is important enough. If you choose not to act, will you be better off a week or month from now, or will things get worse? If you don't act, can your needs be met?

If the situation is important to you, go on to the second question: Is it possible to change this situation?

If you are responding with a high-S or high-C dimension, you may feel that you can't. Maybe yes, maybe no.

You bring many abilities and strengths to this situation, and so do other people. When examining whether it is possible to change the situation, try thinking not about whether *you* can easily change it, but about whether *anyone* could change it. Is this Mission Impossible?

If not, ask the third question: If it is possible to change this situation, is it worth the effort and risk involved?

To answer this question, you may have to work ahead to options 2 and 3, to see what those efforts and risks might be. Perhaps you already know that this is not the time for you to be working on this situation. Then forget it and drive on.

Remember, though, that situations are always evolving. As things change, you may decide that action has become worth it. So it's good to keep an open file on the situation.

Also consider whether the alternatives to taking action are acceptable to you. Let's say that you are stuck in a situation with a difficult person. Will you tiptoe around the person, being overly polite and cautious? Will you do everything you can to not work with that person? Will you wait until tensions build, then explode?

Option 2: Take Action within Your Preferred Style of Behavior

If you've decided to take some action, begin by looking for ways in which you can use your special strengths to resolve the problem. Don't approach a problem by assuming that your response pattern is the problem.

When you are drawing on your high dimension, you are in your comfort zone. You can be you. That's one reason we like some people especially well—we can be ourselves around them, and they like us anyway!

Your high dimension may be just what's needed to resolve the situation. Here's an example. A project is falling behind schedule. At first glance, this would seem to be a situation that could best be addressed by a high-D response that push, push, pushes things forward. Maybe, maybe not. You are responding to the situation with a strong C dimension. How might high-C behavior help this situation? Use your ability to think things through, to analyze closely, and to formulate rules and procedures. You may discover that the tasks have been assigned and ordered carelessly, that sequences of steps don't mesh, that one person is forced to wait for another to complete work before proceeding. You may discover that problems are resulting from trying to push forward too fast. In an atmosphere of frantic activity, errors are being made, requiring steps to be repeated. Your C style may be just what is needed. You can help set procedures and rules that will streamline and accelerate the project.

DiSC focuses on the positive, and you should, too. Be proud. Celebrate your strengths. Broadcast them to others. Volunteer for the kind of work you like best. Help where you want to help. Create an assignment where you can shine.

Talk to other people about what you need to do things your way. After taking DiSC, a budget analyst hung this sign outside his door: "No facts, no figures, no service." He knew that high-C was how a budget analyst had to act, and he wasn't going to apologize for that anymore.

There are strengths in every response pattern. If you go back to the section about your response pattern, you'll find assets you can bring to this situation.

Use your strengths in creative ways—no dimension has an exclusive on creativity.

Also, whatever your high dimension, you have skills, knowledge, and experience of many kinds. Draw on them, too.

Choosing option 2 allows you to play from your strongest position. You can make a contribution while still staying in your comfort zone.

Do share information about how you like to work—and how you do *not* like to work. Try presenting this information in the form of a plan for getting a job done better and faster: "My strengths are . . . but I'm less good at . . ."

Organizations need people who think, feel, and behave in many ways. Perhaps your way is what this situation needs.

Option 3: Adapt

Adapting is choosing a different response because you want to meet the needs of a situation. By adapting, you respond in a way that is less typical for you. It may feel a bit uncomfortable, but you think it will better serve your needs and those of others.

For example, Ann was in charge of a project that she was anxious to move forward. She was having a high-D response and wanted to push people hard. Perhaps, she thought, I should call a team meeting and light some fires under people. Then she remembered what happened the last time the group rushed through a complex project like this one. The results were, well, mediocre. She realized that, for the good of the project, she needed to give a high-C team member the time she needed to complete a quality check. With effort, she adapted and summoned up some patience—because the goal was important to her.

Adapting can be especially worthwhile if you want to improve a key work relationship, for example, with your boss. Let's say you work for someone who tends to respond with a high D. You tend to respond as a high S. Instead of asking your high-D boss to start behaving in a supportive manner, you decide, in certain situations, to adapt beyond your own S-dimension comfort zone and show a willingness to move a bit faster, to take on more responsibility for decision making, and to act more independently.

While you should not assume you're the cause of a problem, it is often a good idea to at least consider whether your response is contributing to it. If it is, it is possible that changing the situation will require adapting.

Not about Changing

Adapting is a conscious decision about behavior, not an attempt to change who you are. It is a practical solution that you choose to meet the needs of the situation.

Old-time vaudeville musicians made a living by being adaptable. They would learn to double on other instruments so they could play them if necessary. A pit-orchestra violinist, for example, would learn to double on brass, meaning that, when necessary, he could play a trumpet, trombone, or tuba. He still played the fiddle most of the time. Doubling on brass did not mean that he had to give up the fiddle.

Similarly, adapting is *not* about changing yourself. It's about adding to your repertoire of behaviors. Drawing on your D dimension does not mean that you have to give up your C-dimension skills. All it means is that, when the situation calls for it, you have developed the ability to "double on D."

Adapting does not mean changing who you are. It is a temporary solution—as are all truly effective solutions, because they address the needs of specific people in specific situations at specific times.

Adapting means you put aside your usual, natural, comfortable way of responding to a situation. Instead, you temporarily use a style that will best meet the needs of the situation. Adapting is possible because, whatever dimension may predominate in you, you have aspects of all four styles within you. You can draw on the less-prominent dimensions to adapt your behavior.

Does adapting seem weak to you? It's the opposite of weak. By adapting, you are taking action.

It Gets Easier

Sometimes a small amount of adapting can make a big difference. So start by thinking about small steps you can make toward meeting the other person's needs. The person may see that you're making an effort, and that can do a lot to ease tension and build a relationship.

Adapting tends to get easier the more you do it, too. If you take small steps at first, you may grow more comfortable with it. In that way, stretching beyond your usual DiSC response is like stretching your muscles. The more you stretch, the more comfortable the moves become and the farther you can go.

Practice adapting *before* you are under a lot of pressure. The next time you approach a routine task and find yourself going about it in a routine manner, consciously consider an alternative approach. "Breaking a habit" is a violent phrase that implies that, once broken, the familiar, comfortable habit is discarded forever. You don't have to break all of your comfortable habits; just, from time to time, look for ways to bend to help you approach the old task from a new perspective. Each habit you bend makes bending the next one that much easier. And yet you shouldn't eliminate behaviors that work for you.

In order to adapt your behavior, you have to be able to tune in to the other person's point of view. DiSC helps here, too. Too often, we go into a situation exclusively focused on getting what we want or, at least, what we think we want. The results are rarely 100 percent satisfactory.

Let's say you learn that you are using a D style in a situation that involves a person who seems to be using an S style. You could try forcing that person to see things your way, to convert from S-ness to D-ness. The result of this emotional wrestling match most likely will be frustration and exhaustion. So you choose to adapt. You look at the situation from a different point of view, and you see what needs to happen.

Adapting in Action

Here's an everyday example of adapting. A co-worker takes you to her favorite restaurant. There is a crowd waiting to be seated. You are about to say something like, "This place must be mismanaged not to be able to handle the lunch traffic." Before you can speak, your co-worker, smiling, says, "This place is *really* popular. I love it! Look at all these people."

Now you have a choice. You can speak your mind, making your co-worker feel bad and possibly starting an argument. Or you can politely agree with your co-worker's observation. That would be nice, but it wouldn't really be you. You might be the one who ends up feeling bad. There is a third alternative, adapting a bit. You might say something like, "Yes, it must be a great place. It's so popular that the management better start thinking about adding a few more waiters and tables!" You have created a common ground between your two points of view. Your response is not offensive to the other person, nor did it require you to give up or suppress your feelings about the situation.

When the stakes are higher, adapting can become much more important. Let's say you are trying to sell your boss on a new computer program for tracking inventory more efficiently. From your point of view, this new system will streamline operations and result in a more efficient organization. These are attitudes typically associated with a high-D style. However, you are aware that your boss tends to have a high-C response. He is meticulous and detail oriented, and likes tried-and-true procedures. Although you're excited about the innovative aspects of the proposed computer program, you decide to adapt. In selling the program to your boss, you emphasize the thorough testing the program has gone through, the fact that most of the industry leaders use the program, and the terrific employee-training course that comes with the program. You explain to your boss the steps you will take to make an orderly, seamless, gradual transition to the new system, which, you add, will build on the current system rather than simply replacing it.

This is adapting. You have temporarily set aside your D-driven feelings in order to appeal to the C-driven feelings of another person. Adapting helps you reach your objective: to persuade your boss to buy and to embrace the new computer program.

You can also choose to adapt when the situation involves not a "difficult task," not a "difficult person." For example, there is a self-employed person who usually responds as a D. But when she has to do her own books, she draws on her C dimension. C isn't her preferred style, but she knows that accounting work requires attention to detail. Her CPA says she does an excellent job and says she wishes everyone was as meticulous. If you asked her how she felt about the work, she might say, "I do it, and I do it well, and when I'm done, I say, 'Thank God I don't have to do that for another quarter!'" Someone else might do this kind of work and say, "Wow, that was really fun!" She does it because she needs to.

Adapting was a very useful strategy for Bill, a sales manager. Bill had trouble working with Tia, who headed the customer-service department. Bill had introduced a series of promotions to stimulate sales, but Tia's department wasn't implementing them effectively. Bill saw Tia as difficult and not open to new ideas. She was really bugging him. One day, as he was telling her about the next promotion, her eyes filled with tears. Suddenly, he started to think about the situation from her point of view. She was feeling stressed about the situation, too. After the meeting, he decided to take a few minutes to reflect on the situation using DiSC. He focused on how he was responding to the launch of the new promotion. Then he used the lists in the People-Reading Signs (chapter 8) to consider how Tia had responded to past promotions. He was responding with high D, and she was responding with high S. He dumped each new promotion on her in a meeting, in front of her staff, and moved quickly to what should be done. Her high-S response was to see the constant flow of new promotions as a source of stress and more work for her staff. She didn't think the promotions were worth all the problems and hard work they were causing.

Bill decided to adapt the way he introduced a promotion. The next time, he talked with her one-on-one. He gave her the rationale behind the program, rather than jumping ahead to what to do. He shared information with her and asked for her help. Then he asked, "What do you need from me to help you implement this?"

Life got a lot better. Tia didn't change, but his interactions with her did.

Here's another true story. Walter, the president of a small company, had repeatedly asked Barry to make some changes in the computer system so it could generate some output he needed. Each time, Barry had bristled. The president decided to use DiSC. He saw that he was asking in a high-D, direct way for what he wanted and that Barry, always analytical and precise, was responding in a high-C way. Barry thought the president was finding a flaw in the system, and he was taking it personally.

Since the D way wasn't being effective, the president decided to adapt his approach. He sent an e-mail that opened with reassurances that he thought the system was great. He then acknowledged that there were lots of things about the system that he didn't know. Walter said he wanted to sit down and talk about the capabilities of the system and how it might generate the needed output. He asked to be educated.

It was the most productive meeting the two had ever had, and it changed the way they worked together. Throughout the meeting, the president made sure to "think C," and particularly to be aware that Barry tended to take comments as criticism. Ultimately, Walter got the reports he needed.

Let's say you are a salesperson who takes a high-D approach to paperwork—you blow through it as fast as you can. The new guy in shipping wants all the shipping forms filled out a certain way, or else. He's been sending your sloppy forms back, delaying shipments to your customers. You observe him for a while, then conclude that he takes a high-C approach to rules and procedures. Your initial, high-D response might be to storm in there and demand some changes. He'd grow defensive. The forms probably still would get booted back—and you wouldn't get the results you want, which is fulfillment of your important orders, on time.

But if you can see his point of view, you might choose instead to relate to the new guy in a way that addresses his high-C needs. You might say, "I appreciate your attention to these shipping forms. Your care means that my customers will get exactly what they ordered. But I need your help with something. Can we develop some sort of system for flagging the hot rush orders like this one?" That will have better results than saying, "Look, I know these forms are important to *you,* but *I* don't have time for a lot of details. This is a hot rush! Get the picture?"

People-reading can help you unstick the situation and get the results you want.

Once you have identified a DiSC dimension as particularly strong in someone, you'll see more clearly what's needed to unstick the situation. Let's say you are writing a sales-pitch letter to a customer you've been having trouble selling on a new line. You observe your previous interactions and conclude that the customer is responding to your sales calls with a high-D. So you put the bottom line on top. Start out the letter with a succinct statement of the goal of your letter and the key information you want the person to know.

Fears

Before you can adapt your behavior, though, you may have to overcome a fear about what may happen. Each of the four dimensions is associated with a particular fear:

- A person responding with a high-D dimension tends to fear loss of control and being taken advantage of. These fears make it uncomfortable to empower others in the situation.
- A person responding with a high-I dimension tends to be afraid of social rejection. This makes it uncomfortable to confront others.
- A person responding with a high-S dimension tends to fear sudden change and personal rejection. This makes it uncomfortable to create change, which will make the situation unstable, while at the same time raising the possibility that people won't like what has been done.
- A person responding with a high-C dimension tends to fear criticism. This makes it uncomfortable to risk being wrong.

How do you move beyond your fears? Recognize them. Name them. Say, "Hello there, fear of losing control. I remember you, old friend. I recognize you, but I'm going to act the way I want to anyway."

By moving beyond your fear, you can choose behavior that is most appropriate or effective for the situation, even if it is not the most comfortable for you. You do what you think is best.

How Adapting Looks to the Other Person

You may be concerned that people will question your motives if you adapt your behavior. Will you come off as inconsistent, two-faced, even manipulative? If you work in a highly competitive or political environment, this might happen. However, most people react quite differently. Without being conscious of the reason, the other person simply feels more comfortable when you use your "adaptive style."

The other person may experience your adaptation several ways, depending on your primary style and his or hers. The person may feel:

- grateful
- respected
- listened to
- thanked
- valued
- relaxed

Here's how one person experienced it: Every morning, Dave charged into his office and got right to work. He never stopped to say good morning to Steve, who worked for him. One day, Dave was annoyed to find that Steve had left for the day right at 4:30. He realized that Steve used to go above and beyond, but not lately.

Dave, who used DiSC regularly, decided to focus on his day-to-day relationship with Steve. He also used the People-Reading Signs and saw that Steve showed a lot of high-S behavior. Dave realized that the personal connection was more important to Steve than it was for him. Dave decided to mentally schedule two minutes when he first got to the office to stop by Steve's desk and ask how his evening or weekend was, or how his allergies were, or whatever.

Did Steve think Dave was being devious? No, he thought Dave was being nice. He felt noticed and appreciated. After a few weeks of this, Dave noticed that Steve was pitching in to help in more ways than ever before. The two minutes invested each morning were paying off big time.

The following sections have some suggestions for ways you might choose to adapt. There are other possibilities in the previous chapter about people-reading.

As you consider these options, think about a situation in your life that has become stuck. Is one of these options the way forward?

Moving from D

Take advantage of the special strengths of the D dimension, but also consider practicing the following ways to adapt:

- identifying with others
- listening to others
- tuning in to the feelings of others
- focusing on the means, not just the ends
- thinking about ways to pace yourself
- thinking about ways to relax from time to time
- heightening your awareness of rules and standards
- being less impulsive
- applying logic and systematic procedures to problems, projects, and activities
- adopting more flexible attitudes toward deadlines
- recognizing the value of planning as well as action

Moving from I

Adapting beyond this dimension requires practicing the following skills:

- managing time effectively
- developing sound systems of organization

- developing a degree of objectivity
- looking more closely at bottom-line profits
- keeping your emotions under control
- developing an analytical approach to data and to procedures
- devoting time and energy to making precise and detailed presentations of information
- developing, where appropriate, a sense of urgency

Moving from S

Here are some areas to consider in moving beyond the S dimension:

- becoming more open to change
- believing your accomplishments are both genuine and worthwhile
- making your accomplishments known to others
- moving projects along more quickly when it is appropriate
- practicing effective presentation skills

Moving from C

To adapt from the C dimension, consider exploring and practicing skills in the following areas:

- making realistic assessments of practical limits
- taking a pragmatic approach to certain issues of quality
- tapping into your intuition
- tolerating conflict
- asking for help or support when you need it
- seeking and appreciating input and explanations from others
- working on teams

Option 4: Dialogue with DiSC

Options 2 and 3, taking action within your preferred style of behavior and adapting your style, are often good choices when you need to act efficiently. The time to act may be *now*. There may be a crisis or a rapidly closing window of opportunity. This is not the best time for a long strategy meeting. In order to avoid or resolve conflict, you decide to act on your own, either using your strengths or adapting to meet the needs of the situation.

When time and circumstances do permit, you may want to choose option 4, which addresses the needs of longer-term situations and working relationships. Option 4 is to begin a dialogue with the other person and to work together to find the best approach to the situation.

DiSC can help open up communications even if the other person hasn't taken the instrument or has never heard of it. You can choose to share what you have learned about yourself and the situation through taking the instrument. Your DiSC knowledge can help you express your feelings and thoughts clearly. Also, DiSC gives you a vocabulary of objective, positive words that can help everyone gain some emotional distance from the situation, particularly if it has escalated into open conflict.

You'll be cutting through the vagueness that often clouds working relationships. Others don't have to guess how you are feeling—you tell them! They don't have to guess what you need in this situation or what it means to you.

You can improve many situations by giving those you work with a heads up concerning areas in which you don't feel comfortable. You're letting others know what pushes your buttons. They'll know better what to expect from you, and they may take certain responses less personally.

You can also find support and understanding in areas where you may be vulnerable. Most people, even those who are not motivated by a high degree of Supportiveness, are willing to help if they perceive that their support will be useful to themselves and the group.

DiSC talk is even more powerful if both people have taken the instrument. Many organizations have given DiSC to everyone on teams, departments, even their whole companies.

If everyone takes the instrument and shares results, people know each other's needs and strengths and can talk in a clear, objective way. People are not put in the awkward position of demanding, "This is what I need." Instead, they are asked to share the results of an instrument that illustrates what each person requires for the group to function best.

It can be hard to talk about the way you've been behaving, let alone share your feelings and thoughts. DiSC can make things less personal and, for most people, more comfortable.

Action Plans and Other Ways to Go about This

You have a lot of options—all the way from choosing to do nothing to initiating a group dialogue!

Depending on the scope and importance of the situation, you may choose an option after just a moment's reflection—but discipline yourself to take that minute. You may want to spend more time reflecting on your options—a few quiet minutes or during a brisk walk.

Many people find it useful to write down their thoughts, particularly if the situation is unfamiliar or complex. You may want to guide your reflections with one of the following action plans. Choose the one that seems most fitting for the situation and for your style.

However, action plans aren't for everybody. Some people work through the process in their heads. Maybe the shower is their thinking place or the drive to work. Some people are intuitive thinkers—they draw, make collages, or sculpt—and answers pop out. Some people like to talk through the situation with their significant other or a trusted colleague.

You are the expert on you and how to best process what you have learned.

MY ACTION PLAN
Choosing an Option

1. Is this situation important to me? Is it possible to change this situation? If it is possible to change this situation, is it worth the effort and risk involved?

2. What strengths do I bring to this situation? How can I act in ways that make the best use of my strengths?

3. What is most needed to improve this situation? How may I choose to adapt to meet these needs?

4. Do I want to initiate a dialogue to resolve this situation? What might I be willing to share?

Personal Insights

➤ What insights have I gained about myself in this situation?

➤ What insights do I have about my relationships with others in this situation?

➤ How might I use the insights I've gained to achieve the results I want?

MY ACTION PLAN
Analyzing the Situation

➤ Have I learned something new that can help me in this situation?

➤ Is there an element of my behavior that may be misunderstood by people in this situation?

➤ What can I do to be more clear in order to avoid misunderstanding?

➤ What other people are important to me in this situation?

➤ What do I want these people to know?

➤ Sometimes a situation requires the passage of time before the issues become clear and action can be taken. Is letting go and accepting the current situation for now possible for me?

➤ How can I move toward the best possible outcome?

MY ACTION PLAN

Someone I Work With

Name and dimension of behavior:

▷ What does that person need most in this situation?

▷ What do I need most in this situation?

▷ What could I do that will meet the other person's needs?

▷ How might I change the situation by adapting my own behavior?

MY ACTION PLAN
Direct Communication

From:

To:

Re: What Is Important to Me

➤ I appreciate having you on our team because:

➤ Here's what you can do to help me be more effective and comfortable in my role on our team:

➤ When people do the following, it makes my role more difficult:

➤ If there is conflict in the group, this is how I'd like the conflict to be resolved:

➤ My number one priority in interacting with you will be:

➤ I'd like your number one priority in interacting with me to be:

Does Your Organization Look Like This?

CHAPTER TEN

When your organization has a problem, you probably know ahead of time how it will react. You also know the atmosphere of the place. Is there a hush in the halls, or do you hear the buzz of conversation, punctuated by bursts of loud laughter? Is the atmosphere charged with competition, or friendly and relaxed? How does the organization treat people? How does it approach tasks? What does it criticize? What does it reward?

Organizations have behavioral styles, too.

While researchers have extensively tested the DiSC instrument with individuals, they have not tested it on the organizational level. Still, the application rings true. Organizational style may not have a research basis, but when you work someplace, you can recognize it.

Where does organizational style come from? In many companies, the top managers—or even one person—set the tone. While it is probably true that if eight out of the ten people in your work group regularly show a high-D dimension, the group's collective style will be marked strongly by Dominance, this may not be the case if the boss and his or her top managers are high-I.

The nature of the organization plays a part, too. What business are you in? A steel plant is a very different place from an advertising agency. Where are you? Big city, suburb, small town, East Coast, West Coast, Midwest, South? Is the company new or is it getting ready to celebrate its fiftieth anniversary? Small or large? Family owned? Fortune 500?

Reading Your Organization

You can't sit your organization down and ask it to take DiSC. Even if you did, the results would not be meaningful because organizational style is not just an average of the styles of the people who work there. However, just as you learned to read other people's styles by observing their behavior, you can read the style of your work environment.

It is still a very good idea for all members of an organization or work group to take the DiSC instrument because this gives everyone a common, precise, nonjudgmental language for communicating feelings and needs. But reading an organization is far less a matter of trying to collate the results of individual DiSC instruments than it is of observing the group as a whole.

The best way to read your organization's style is to ask three questions:

- What does the organization model or present to its members as the right or desirable way to do things?
- What does the organization reward?
- What does the organization criticize?

Think about these questions as you read through the following sections about each style. Ask yourself: Does my organization behave this way?

As always, it is best to focus on a specific situation. In certain situations, an organization's collective style may be, say, high-D while in other situations, the S dimension may shine.

Depending on size and other factors, organizations can be very diverse. It is quite possible that none of these groups of descriptive phrases and terms will describe your organization perfectly. More than one DiSC dimension may be high. Use the descriptions as guides to help you identify at least some of the leading qualities of your organization. The result *may* be a moment of brilliant revelation; but, more likely it will be a set of words that can help you to think about your organization and how you can work most effectively within it.

Observing your organization's style can help you answer questions like these:

- What can I do to help this organization perform more effectively?
- How can I use my special strengths most effectively in this organization?
- In what areas are misunderstandings about me most likely to develop?
- How might I adapt my behavior to improve the way I am perceived in this organization and the way I work within it?
- Is this organization likely to give me messages of value?
- Is there a gap between what I need and what the organization needs? How might I close this gap?
- Will this organization *ever* be right for me—and vice versa?

Signs of a D Organization

Consider the following phrases:

- Decisions are made quickly.
- Innovation is praised.
- The company wants to be there first, with the most.
- People are direct, even blunt.
- People don't seem to get into trouble when they break the rules.
- There are many chiefs and would-be chiefs.
- Things really happen around here!
- It's competitive.
- People use a lot of high-power sports analogies (let's go for the touchdown, that was a real slam dunk, I really spiked it, etc.).
- Risk-takers rise in the organization.
- People tend to act first, ask questions later (or never).
- Perks and status symbols matter.

The collective feel of this workplace can include self-confidence, decisiveness, risk-taking, pressure to achieve, lack of concern for others, impatience, and impulsiveness.

If many of these words and statements describe your organization, you can assume that you are working in a predominantly D-dimension group.

Exhibit D

A consultant who often uses DiSC in his programs has a friend named Ted. Ted called him one afternoon, all excited about a Website he'd been working on. It was an on-line newsletter for day traders—the new army of mostly amateur stock traders who specialize in buying and selling a given stock typically on the same day and, sometimes, within a few hours or even minutes. It's a fast-moving, high-risk, and nerve-racking business, and Ted figured that day traders would be willing to pay for whatever good guidance and hot tips they could get. He had assembled a team of three writers besides himself, all very intense traders, and added to that an editor to help put the publication together.

"Sounds like quite a team," the friend remarked.

"Well," Ted laughed, "*team* may be too optimistic a word. We all just write, e-mail our work to the editor, then yell at him when he takes too long to put it all together."

"You *yell* at him?"

"I'm afraid so. He gets pretty frustrated, too. Complains that we're inconsistent, that we contradict each other, that we misspell things, that we leave out punctuation. But, look, the name of this game is speed. Day-trade stuff gets old before it's even new."

"Well," the friend remarked, "I understand. But hollering at someone each time he does his job probably isn't a very effective management technique. . . ."

"Look, that's just the way this business is. Each of us who writes for the newsletter has a certain way of doing things. Probably the only thing we have in common is that, whatever we do, we do it fast. I *know* we need an editor, but if this guy can't take the heat, well, he'll just have to get out. Let's just say that none of us has much time to be nice."

The friend checked out the Website and the newsletter. It looked splashy and bursting with information. The friend didn't know much about the world of day trading, so he couldn't tell whether the advice was good or bad. It sure was hard to read, though: strange wording, sentence fragments, misspelled words. It looked like it had been put together fast.

After looking at the Website, the friend decided he owed it to Ted to talk with him. He understood that the four writers were high-D in this situation. They were decisive about their advice, and they wanted to get it out fast. They were not interested in pausing along the way to tidy up the details. Wisely, they had hired an editor to do this—probably someone most comfortable in a high-C environment. Unfortunately, they were not using the editing talent they had hired. He was on board, but he was never part of the team, and it was clear that the others considered him an obstacle on the way to their goal. This resulted in a newsletter that was hard to read and that was peppered with grammatical errors. It didn't look buttoned-up, which is how a lot of people like their financial advice to be. Also, the editor was probably pretty angry about how he was being treated.

A few days later, the friend called Ted back and suggested that he and his team of writers give the editor at least a *little* more time and latitude to clean up after them.

Ted said, "We're way ahead of you."

"Oh, great!"

"Yeah. We no longer have an editor."

"What? You let him go?"

"Well, he sort of quit." Ted paused. "And that's fine. He went his way, we went ours. It lets us get the newsletter posted much faster."

The friend knew that this was not the time to deliver a lecture about how an organization can benefit from a variety of DiSC styles. As the writers saw it, everyone now involved in the enterprise shared at least one goal: *Get the newsletter out fast.* Whether their audience would continue to purchase a 100 percent high-speed, high-D product, warts and all, remained to be seen.

Signs of an I Organization

Consider the following phrases:

- Folks are friendly and upbeat.
- There's lots of socializing and small talk.

- It's a fun place.
- People call meetings all the time, and they tend to run over schedule.
- There aren't a lot of procedures and rules.
- It's okay to skim over the details.
- There are recognition programs and awards.
- Pitches and presentations are big deals, and you're admired if you can do them well.
- The office parties are fun.

In this workplace, you'll find enthusiasm, charm, sociability, easy expression of emotion, impulsiveness, disorganization, and a lack of follow-through. If many of these words and phrases describe your organization, you can assume that you are working in a predominantly I-dimension group.

Exhibit I

"So, have you sold your house yet?" Susan asked Martha.

"Well, it's been close to selling several times now. At least that's what the agency says."

"What agency?"

Martha named one Susan knew by reputation. "They're supposed to be fantastic. John and Tascha sold their house through them. They say they've got a real 'can do' attitude. Very *up*."

Martha continued, "That's sure the feeling in their office. They're very *positive* about everything. The enthusiasm is contagious. And they're *all* like that, from the receptionist to each of the agents I spoke with. Everything's 'no problem' with them. You know, I was concerned about the fact that the house has only two bedrooms, while the others in the neighborhood have at least three, or even four or five. The agent said that was no problem. 'We'll position it like a sleek sports car,' one of the other agents said to me. 'You wouldn't want a sports car with four doors, would you? So, we'll make two bedrooms *more* appealing than four.' I have to admit, I was impressed. I suppose I should have asked just how they were going to go about promoting the two bedrooms this way. But I didn't.

"Anyway, they keep telling me we're close to a sale. To tell you the truth, I'm getting discouraged. Sometimes I just want to take my agent by her neck and tell her just to give it to me straight. *Why isn't the house selling?*"

"Are you sure they aren't being realistic?" Susan asked.

"Well, they haven't sold the house, and it's been on the market for almost three months."

"That doesn't mean their optimism is faked. Sounds to me like the whole organization values a sunny outlook, even if it doesn't always quite reflect reality. I can understand why you're getting impatient with them. There is nothing more frustrating than being fed good news but no results."

"Maybe I should just fire them."

"Maybe. But optimism is valuable in a sales organization. I mean, it's great that these folks are persuasive and that they won't give up."

"But how can I keep working with them if I can't get a clear picture of reality?"

"Tell them what you want. Just begin by letting them know that they're doing a great job and that you really appreciate the way they keep up a high level of enthusiasm about the property. Then let them know that you need feedback from the prospects. What do they like? What don't they like? Based on this, maybe you can decide if a price adjustment is called for."

"I don't know. I just don't think I can get these people to change. You know, they're all *up* all of the time, and that inflated optimism just gets reinforced, because they're all like that."

"Don't try to change them. You won't succeed, and, in any case, you *want* that enthusiasm. Just let your agent know what information you want from her. You want the optimism and enthusiasm directed at the prospects, not at you. But don't discourage them. Let them know that they're doing a great job, that the enthusiasm of their organization is worth its weight in gold. Get the objectivity you need by asking for a report with some straightforward feedback."

Signs of an S Organization

Consider the following phrases:

- There are few chiefs and many followers.
- Open conflict is rare.
- People sound genuine when they ask, "How are you doing?"
- There's quiet conversation.
- The pace is easygoing, even slow.
- Loyalty is valued.
- People enjoy working on teams.
- Folks are nice to each other.
- People accomplish tasks by cooperating with others.
- They are good listeners.
- When changes are announced, people look stunned.
- People talk about "the good of the group."

This workplace is where you'll see people displaying patience, being obliging, and thinking of others even more than themselves. If most of these words and phrases describe your organization, you can assume that you are working in a predominantly S-dimension group.

Exhibit S

Mary had left a position as an accountant with a small but aggressive publisher to take over the accounting department of a local branch of a national community service organization.

She had made the move for what might best be described as spiritual reasons. That is, she wanted to be part of a community-oriented, life-improving enterprise. In this, she was not disappointed. The first few weeks at the new place were exhilarating. Not only was she with an organization that was doing immensely satisfying work, but the people she worked with were supportive, caring, sensitive, and considerate. Not that the folks in the small publishing house had been bad or even unpleasant, but they were all business, always narrowly focused on wresting profits from publishing specialized books in a very competitive market. Small talk? How's the family? Seen any good movies lately? No time for any of that there. The office didn't even have a coffeemaker.

"What a change," Mary told a friend over lunch one day. "These people really care about each other—not just as co-workers, but as *people*. You know, my dog Max gets terrible skin allergies every summer. He really suffers, and the scratching is incessant. Drives us all crazy. So I mentioned Max's allergies during a coffee break at work. They take a lot of coffee breaks. Actually, they're usually tea breaks. A bunch of them are into herbal teas of all kinds, which they share with everyone.

"Well, poor Max became the focus of conversation. Everyone had an idea for a remedy, and one person even gave me the name of a veterinary allergist. I didn't even know there were such things! Every day now, at least two or three people ask me how Max is doing. *Is he any better, poor thing?* That's the kind of place it is."

Some weeks later, Mary was speaking less enthusiastically about her new job. "I really like the people, but sometimes, I have to admit, they get on my nerves. Every step that is proposed becomes the subject of a separate meeting. Always a very *polite* meeting. 'Is this good for you? Are you sure doing this won't intrude on your turf?' That kind of thing. In many ways, it's gratifying to be among people who are just so considerate. But it's almost impossible to get anything done. For example, I need to put in place the financial reporting software we're going to be using, and I need to get it up and running before the fiscal year starts. But because everyone will be using this software, it's become the subject of endless discussion. 'Well, it works for me,' one of them will say. 'But wasn't the old software better for everyone else?' And so it goes."

After a few more weeks on the job, Mary was happy again. Her friend had been worried about her when they last talked, so Mary called her with an update.

"You know, I've finally figured out how to work with these people. To begin with, whenever I feel like I'm going to lose it—I mean, just blow my patience entirely—I stop and think about why I took this job to begin with. It *is* a good organization, and it does important work that really makes a difference in our community. So I remind myself that ultimate satisfaction is worth a little frustration.

"Here's something else I've discovered. These people haven't set out to frustrate me. In fact, that's the last thing they'd want to do. I was getting annoyed by all the time being wasted with expressions of concern for each other, 'Is this okay with you?' or 'I wanted to check with you before I did anything.' And so on.

"Then I realized that what I was seeing was a genuine desire throughout the whole organization to be supportive.

I mean, that's what our work is all about, and that's also the way these people treat one another.

"So now, when I need a fast decision or I need information right away, I put it like this: 'It would help me if you made your decision by the end of the week. That would be a great help.' I used to say, 'We really, really need this decision by Friday.' Nine times out of ten, that would produce sheer paralysis. But if I ask for help, for support—well, that seems to loosen the gears. I still may not get a decision exactly on time, but at least I *do* get a decision.

"These are very good people, who are doing a good job. I'm not going to change them. I wouldn't want to change them even if I could. I've discovered that what I *can* do is meet them halfway, and what happens is this: I get things done about half as fast as I did at the publishing house, but that's twice as fast as these folks got things done before *I* came on board!"

Signs of a C Organization

Consider the following phrases:

- The organization has high standards.
- People are rewarded for lavishing attention on detail.
- They value analytical thinking.
- They demand accuracy.
- Performance expectations are clearly defined.
- There's a place for everything, and everything is in its place.
- Conversations tend to be guarded.
- Tasks are approached methodically.
- There are plans and contingency plans and just-in-case plans.
- People use phrases like "risk management," "paper trail," and "quality control."

- The atmosphere is businesslike.
- There may be a formal or understood dress code.

The collective feel can be cautious, restrained, perfectionist, critical, or proper. If most of these words and phrases adequately describe your organization, you can assume that you are working in a predominantly C-dimension group.

Exhibit C

A small firm makes and markets special accessories for amateur astronomers. The company sells to a small, highly specific market niche—and does okay at it. One day, Bob Simpson, the firm's only salesman, decided that "doing okay" wasn't enough. By listening to his customers, he had learned a lot about their needs. One problem kept coming up over and over. It seemed that focusing a small telescope by hand often created a problem. Even mounted on a sturdy tripod, most telescopes jiggled and vibrated when the focusing knob was turned. Frequently, this was enough to knock the star or planet being viewed right out of the telescope's field of view. Very frustrating. It would be great, several customers told Bob, if his company could come up with a remote-control motorized focuser that would turn the focus knob at the touch of a button, without shaking the telescope.

That seemed like a perfect product. Bob talked to Ed Charles, the CEO. Ed, like the rest of the half-dozen employees, is an engineer. He responded to Bob's idea the way most engineers would respond—by bombarding him with a series of highly specific questions: "What will the power source be?" "What kind of motor will we use?" "What kinds of coupling will work with which kinds of telescopes?" And so on.

Bob just sat there. Finally he said, "Look, I just thought it was a good idea. Do *you* think it's a good idea?"

Ed wouldn't volunteer a yes or no. By way of response, he just said, "Let's call a meeting—get everyone in on it." He looked at his electronic organizer. "Are you free at 10:45 on Wednesday the 22nd?"

With his customary high enthusiasm, Bob presented his idea to the engineers, concluding with, "So, what do you think? Great idea, huh?"

What followed was a series of questions, much like those Ed had asked, only a lot more of them.

Bob held up his hands like a traffic cop. The questions stopped.

In the silence that followed, Bob was about to tell the others just to forget it. After all, the company was doing okay without a remote-control focuser. But instead of giving up, he decided to try talking to the engineers in the language they spoke—or, at least, as close as he could get to it.

"I understand," he said, "that we need to formulate very exact specs for this project. That is where you'll come in. But, first, let me tell you *exactly* what I can tell you.

"Number one, customers want a remote-control focuser.

"Number two, it needs to be adaptable to a wide range of telescopes. I don't know how many we can accommodate. That is something we need to find out. I will make a note of that. But I do know that the more we can fit, the more of these focusers we'll sell.

"Number three, just by talking with customers, I know that they are willing to pay as much as $150 for this thing. So there's our target retail price point.

"Right now, those are the facts I can give you. Let me suggest some first steps you folks can take to get us started from this point:

"First, inventory all of the technical risks and road-blocks. Can they be overcome? How?

"Second, inventory the patent issues. I'm not aware of

anything like this currently available. But we'd better take an overview before we get too deeply involved."

It was difficult for Bob to say these things. To him, it was like trying to speak in Greek. Driven by a very high-I dimension, he was far more excited by broad concepts than by the details. When details were demanded of him, his first impulse was to withdraw, but then he realized that he was trying to communicate with a group of high-C engineers. They wanted—they *needed*—details, facts. Bob decided to give them what they wanted, at least as much as he *could* give them. The facts he had at his command were pretty meager, but he presented them in as orderly and complete a fashion as he could. Now, having done that, he let the engineers know that all of the other facts would have to come from them—the people who were most adept at working with such material.

As Bob faced this group of people, he realized that they simply looked at the world quite differently from the way he did. There was a moment of frustration and something like despair, but then he realized that this fact did not mean that he was obliged to transform himself into something he was not. Nor did he have to try to transform everyone else. Least of all did he have to walk away and quit. Instead, he decided to give the engineers as much as he could, then let *them* take it from there, using the techniques and procedures they knew best and letting *them* ask and answer the questions that were relevant to them.

At last, Ed Charles looked at Bob: "I think we're all agreed that this idea has potential. Let's get to work on it. This meeting is over."

Action?

After you have made some determinations about the style of your organization, what should you do?

You have the same four options you had after learning to read an individual person's style. You can choose to:

1. Do nothing.
2. Take action, but remain within your preferred dimension of behavior.
3. Adapt your behavior to meet the needs of the organization.
4. Engage in a dialogue with the others in the organization.

It's important to point out that you do not need to have the same style as your organization to fit in. In fact, if you usually display a different style you may bring much needed balance. However, the differences may make things uncomfortable for you sometimes.

It is possible that you may ultimately decide to part ways with this particular group. You would hardly be alone in such a decision. According to the U.S. Bureau of Labor Statistics, the average worker these days changes employers no fewer than seven times during his or her working life—and changes *careers* three times. But don't be in a hurry to make your escape just because your predominant style differs from that of the group. Your may bring a fresh point of view and a special strength to the enterprise. Conversely, experience in an environment that contrasts with your comfort zone can inspire you to develop new strengths and your ability to adapt.

Closing Words: It's Up to You

"**C**an I have a copy to take home for my husband/wife?" is something DiSC trainers hear often.

In this book, we've stayed in the workplace, but you can choose to use DiSC in other parts of your life, too. You can use DiSC wherever and whenever it is important to clarify what you and others feel, need, and want.

Relationships with friends, family, and significant others are at least as complex as business relationships. Different points of view can lead to misunderstandings and conflict. Certainly, personal relationships are charged with all kinds of emotions and benefit from good communication.

You may want to introduce a family member or friend to this book and share your results with each other. Make sure to let the person know that there are no right or wrong answers. This is not a magazine quiz that will reveal that you and your partner are all wrong for each other. It is a way to talk about things that matter to each of you, with a safe and precise vocabulary that facilitates good communication.

Many people have found DiSC useful in their volunteer work. Volunteer work tends to throw together people of diverse response styles. They may have been drawn to the organization for many different reasons, to fill their own needs. Once there, volunteers often feel that because they are not being paid for their work, the organization should be accommodating and should respect their ways of doing things. Moreover, few organizations interview and select

IF YOU WERE A PARENT ARRIVING FOR YOUR CHILD'S CONCERT:

- **D RESPONSE: STAY ON THE CELL PHONE UP TO CONCERT TIME**
- **I RESPONSE: VOLUNTEER TO GREET OTHER PARENTS AND HAND OUT THE PROGRAMS**
- **S RESPONSE: ARRIVE EARLY SO YOUR CHILD CAN SEE YOU SITTING IN THE FRONT ROW**
- **C RESPONSE: ARRIVE EARLY TO SET UP YOUR VIDEO CAMERA ON A TRIPOD**

volunteers whose styles will mesh well with the group's—they're just happy to have a volunteer. If you are in a leadership position in such an organization, consider using DiSC to facilitate collaboration on a particular project or on an ongoing basis.

In fact, DiSC can be a useful tool in any situation when calm deliberation is called for but is in short supply. The unthreatening language of DiSC can help defuse the situation and open up a dialogue.

There is a special version of DiSC just for teenagers, called I-Sight. It's in a program used in many schools and is included in a book for teens called *Knowing Me, Knowing You*, published by Inscape and Free Spirit Publishing. Young people often have trouble putting their thoughts and feelings into words. DiSC can help them see that while they may not be able to choose how they feel, they can choose how to act on those feelings. For young people, this can be a liberating revelation.

DiSC is your tool. It is a tool with a lifetime warranty, guaranteed never to wear out. May it help you break through stuck situations to good relationships, successful outcomes, and satisfaction in your work and in your life.

Remember:

- Don't label yourself or others.
- Take baby steps.
- Take yourself off automatic pilot.
- Keep on being the expert on you.

The Combination DiSC Patterns

DI
ACTIVE AND LEADING

If your tallies for D *and* I are both 44 or higher, in this situation you have a DI response pattern. (The DI pattern is not the same as the ID pattern. If both your D and I scores are high, but your I score is *higher,* go to the next section, "ID: Expressive and Involved.")

In this situation, you are feeling confident and know you can get the job done. You probably believe that you have high visibility and influence in this situation. You want to move quickly and single-mindedly toward your goal. You put a lot of energy into your work.

Value to the Group

You are gravitating toward a leadership role. If you can't lead, you want to make sure your views are at least heard. While people who respond with a Dominance style are content to go their own way, those who add a strong Influence

DI Style

What motivates you?
- Leading
- Setting your own course
- Moving quickly
- Making decisions

What discourages you?
- Detailed directions or instructions
- Putting up with circumstances you don't like
- Lack of opportunity to lead, speak up, or share your ideas
- Not being where the action is

What is your favorite environment?
- Common interests and goals
- Status
- High visibility
- Open communication

What do you avoid?
- Strict rules and regulations
- Detailed, slow-paced projects
- Isolation
- Negativity

dimension perform best when they share the group's vision and goals.

You may be perceived as a "strong personality," which both you and the group consider a compliment.

Areas of Misunderstanding

Others call you *driven*. When the goal is in sight, you lock in. All your buttons are pushed at once, and your energy surges. You refuse to quit until you reach the goal. Other people find this either admirable or exhausting. People may get tired of trying to keep up with you and lose interest in the project.

If your energy, determination, and focus have outlasted those of others, you may be tempted to say, "I'll do it myself." Independent initiatives can be valuable for you and the group, but they can distance you from your colleagues. Plus, the extra hours can wear even you out.

Watch out for these areas of possible conflict:

- a tendency to dismiss the feelings of others if things don't move fast enough or decisively enough to suit you
- a tendency to act impulsively
- the risk of becoming so intensely competitive that you stop cooperating with others

Information to Share

You may find it helpful in this situation to share some insights about how you work best.

Let people know that you like to do things your own way and, for that reason, may seem impatient when given detailed instructions. Tell people that you love to be innovative. You thrive when you are allowed to find new approaches to solving problems.

When tasks are divvied up, ask for the tasks you think are most important—that's where you work hardest and best.

After you and the group agree on a goal, consider dividing tasks so that you can work more or less independently. But *do* make sure that everyone is on the same page before you throw yourself into the task.

What to Look Out For

Because you are self-directed, energetic, and not easily discouraged, people may tend to follow your lead. If those followers can't keep up with you, you may feel disappointed and even angry. This can harm the group's productivity and morale. People may start to view you not as charmingly direct, but as overly demanding.

Getting Unstuck

Situation: You're starting to feel like a leader without any followers.

Possibility: You may not feel the need for feedback on how a project is going, but ask for it anyway. This is a good way to keep others involved, and it will help you gauge the strength of their commitments. People want to know that you are concerned about their feelings and ideas.

Situation: The results weren't what you were hoping for.

Possibility: Along the way, try to be more open to the ideas of others.

Situation: You do everything yourself.

Possibility: Before succumbing to the I'll-do-it-myself syndrome, first consider whether you can reach the goal better by inspiring others to work with you.

Your Bottom Line

When you respond with a DI style, you act boldly and express yourself directly. This can be just the thing a group needs to get out of the mud. Your work will be most productive when you and the group share the same goals. To make sure everyone agrees on overall objectives and goals, do plenty of talking—and even more listening. Open yourself up to other people's ideas. You like to go your own way, but be sure to consider the input of others.

This Combination in Action

Sarah was determined not to let it happen again.

Last year, when she had been put in charge of an advertising campaign for a new shoe polish, she went all out. Enthusiastic about the product, she designed a major, expensive campaign with television and radio spots as well as color print ads. She put a lot of creative energy into the campaign. She finished it in record time—partly because of her own high energy, partly because she didn't "waste time" seeking feedback from other people.

The big day came. She made her presentation to the client: TV spots, radio ads, newspaper and magazine ads, and maybe even an infomercial.

The client's jaw dropped.

I've wowed him, Sarah thought. Just look at this guy. He hardly knows what to say.

What he said was, "You know, it's only shoe polish."

In her enthusiasm, Sarah had given the client much more than he expected, wanted, or was willing to pay for. Embarrassed, she looked on while her boss and the client put their heads together to pare the campaign down to a few black-and-white newspaper ads and a number of fifteen-second radio spots.

On the plus side, because Sarah had insisted on doing it all herself, no one else's time had been wasted in concocting something this customer didn't want. But she could have saved her own time and energy if she had invested a few minutes asking questions and making sure everyone shared the same objectives.

Now, handed the assignment of working up an ad campaign for a new kind of pencil eraser, Sarah leapt right in, began to think about some big TV commercials—then came to an abrupt stop.

I need a good long meeting with the client first, she said to herself.

She pushed her chair back from her computer, reached for the phone, and dialed the client's number.

ID
EXPRESSIVE AND INVOLVED

The previous profile described the DI response pattern. The ID pattern also combines D and I—both scores are at or above 44—but covers situations in which your tally for I is *greater than* that for D. The differences are dramatic. The DI style is *goal-driven*, but the ID style is *relationship-driven*.

If you have an ID response to your focus situation, you are expressing your feelings freely and others are responding warmly. You do not shy away from challenging interpersonal situations, because you know that you are good at resolving conflicts and making things better for everyone.

Value to the Group
You can be the spark plug of a work group. You get involved, volunteering ideas and encouraging others to do the same. You are very enthusiastic, especially when the work is on the cutting edge.

ID Style

What motivates you?

- Building strong working relationships
- Generating support for new challenges
- Contributing to the success of the group
- Direct responsibility for outcomes

What discourages you?

- Routine tasks and procedures
- Little interaction with others
- Dull people

What is your favorite environment?

- Exciting new projects
- Open conflict-resolution
- Recognition for your efforts

What do you avoid?

- Conflict
- Inflexible rules
- Detailed or in-depth analysis
- Questioning of your ideas or judgment

While you're a positive person, you're not afraid of conflict because you have the communications skills to resolve sticky situations.

Areas of Misunderstanding

Enthusiasm, when it is well-founded, is extraordinarily valuable to any group. In a situation to which you respond with a strong ID pattern, you may well be in a position to rally support for a new idea or project.

What's wrong with being so up? You are *so* positive and *so* well-liked that some people may think you're just looking for attention, status, or authority. While you like to get credit when it's due, you don't have ulterior motives. You're just enthusiastic, plain and simple; some people will refuse to believe you don't have a hidden agenda.

Information to Share

You are easy to get along with, and you readily adapt to a wide variety of jobs and work situations. Nevertheless, three situations present special difficulty for you:

- inflexible rules
- detailed or in-depth analysis
- questioning of your ideas or judgment

Let your co-workers know that you perform best when you don't have to follow a great many rules and cookie-cutter procedures. You have both the ability and the desire to direct your own work.

What to Look Out For

Because you like to move quickly, you can help your group overcome inertia and go forward. However, you can create problems if you skim *too* lightly over the surface of issues. You may resist looking too closely if you think you'll find a problem or point of disagreement that could slow down the work.

When problems or disputes do surface, you rush to solve them. In some situations, this can be a plus, but others may think you fail to understand the complexities of the problem or the seriousness of the issues. They may think you are downplaying the problem or even covering it up. It is important to resolve issues efficiently and promptly, but it is equally important that others feel their concerns are heard.

If you had a straight D style, it wouldn't bother you too much if others felt you didn't care about their ideas or their problems. But the ID response means you are concerned about relationships, even valuing them above goals and achievements.

Sometimes, the task requires patience and attention to detail. Enthusiasm isn't always what a particular situation requires.

Getting Unstuck

Situation: People think you're arrogant.
Possibility: Let others know that you think success depends on everyone. You'll feel better if you take the time to bring them on board.

Situation: The project was derailed because you had overlooked an important detail.
Possibility: Always eager to move forward, you might overlook an important detail or two. You might want to ask someone to check your work from time to time. This may be difficult for you, but it can save your "you know what."

Your Bottom Line

Enthusiasm is contagious. Just don't let yours be mistaken for showboating.

This Combination in Action

Bill had built his reputation in sales as someone who closes his deals. The sales director gave him the hottest prospects because he knew that Bill combined the enthusiasm of a cheerleader with the stamina of a marathon runner.

Understandably, Bill liked getting the most promising leads. He liked earning the commissions, but, even more, he enjoyed being a star. What was wrong with *this* picture?

Lately, Bill had the feeling that his co-workers weren't happy to see him. Most conversations were those he started. People had stopped asking him how he was doing.

Bill understood what was going on. Lately, he was being given all the hot leads, while most of the other salespeople spent their time making low-percentage cold calls.

Well, thought Bill, somebody's got to make the cold calls.

True enough. Cold calls—calling up perfect strangers—were a source of new leads. Unfortunately, for every cold call that results in a sale down the road, a hundred produce only frustration and fatigue. Cold calling is tough, unglamorous work. Bill knew that his sales record had earned him a ticket out, but he realized that those around him resented his stardom and resented being saddled with all the dirty work. He set up a meeting with his sales director.

"Mary," he said, "I know this sounds crazy, but I feel the need to do some of the cold calling."

After Mary picked her jaw up off the floor, she gave Bill a short list of names. From then on, he spent part of two days out of every week making cold calls. As he had expected, the work was dull and disappointing, but his co-workers started talking to him again, and for Bill, it was worth it.

DS
SELF-MOTIVATED AND HELPFUL

If, in your focus situation, your tallies for D and S are both at or above 44, your response pattern is DS, whether the D or the S tally is higher.

Dominance and Supportiveness seem to be opposites. If, in this situation, you are using a DS style, does that mean you're contradicting yourself? No. It means there is flexibility built into your pattern. In this situation, you are trying to maintain the inner direction of the D style while remaining supportive of others. You are balancing your determined, decisive, sometimes even impatient drive with a strong desire to be helpful.

While you don't need to be wildly popular, you think it is important and *satisfying* to work well with others. You want to define and achieve certain goals, but you also want to benefit others.

Because you are both self-motivated *and* helpful, you are motivated by opportunities to balance independent work with fruitful collaboration.

While people who demonstrate a single D response pattern accept, even welcome, conflict and aggressive competition, you don't.

Value to the Group

A person having this response pattern gets along well with others but isn't dependent on them. You are probably a self-

DS Style

What motivates you?

▷ Personal commitment to the goal

▷ A balance of independent work and collaboration

▷ Keeping things moving

▷ Personal accountability

What discourages you?

▷ When people's feelings don't count

▷ When quality is ignored

▷ Open conflict

▷ Aggressive competition

What is your favorite environment?

▷ Clear direction with group support

▷ Doing the job well counts

▷ Respect for diverse needs

What do you avoid?

▷ Asking for help, even when it is needed

▷ Answering a lot of questions about your decisions or approach

▷ Embarrassment

starter, designing your own approach to most tasks and problems. As your co-workers begin to associate you with good outcomes, they will give you their appreciation and, even, their loyalty.

Areas of Misunderstanding

As you balance D and S, you may surprise some people. You're self-motivated, determined, and risk-taking, and also friendly, helpful, and considerate. A colleague who picks up on one aspect of your pattern can be surprised when the other dimension comes to the front. He or she may even feel blindsided.

Others may not understand why you want to work alone. It's not that you don't feel loyal to the group; it's just that you don't want to work side by side.

Information to Share

Let others know that, although you often prefer to work alone, you *are* a team player. Even when you're working on your own, you always keep the group's best interests in mind.

As a self-motivated individual, you are your harshest— but also most useful—critic. You'd rather judge results for yourself than hear feedback from others, though you usually listen patiently when it's given. While it is not a good idea to ask others to keep their opinions to themselves, you don't have to ask for feedback you do not really want.

What to Look Out For

It is not always easy to balance the contrasting elements of your response pattern. While you are self-directed and guided by high *personal* performance standards, you also feel that everything you do should be in the best interests of the group. Consequently, you may think you're letting *others* down if you don't do *your* best. It is great to take personal responsibility for your actions, but you may feel a lot of stress if you let others down. Here are some ways to regain your balance:

- Realize that you are harder on yourself than anyone else is.
- Resist the temptation to shoulder the burdens of the entire group.
- Look to your colleagues and co-workers for support. They *will* give it to you.
- Consider really *listening* to some of the feedback you get. You'll probably find that other people appreciate your work more than you do!

Getting Unstuck
Situation: You're doing it all alone.
Possibility: Give others the chance to help you. Force yourself to delegate what you can.

Situation: You are your toughest critic.
Possibility: Listening to the feedback of others can help you gain perspective and ease your stress.

Your Bottom Line
It may never occur to you that you could benefit from anyone's help. This is a strength when you need to work intensively by yourself. Many group members will appreciate your initiative, as it frees them to get other work done. Just don't let your independence go too far. Sometimes asking for help is the fastest, most efficient, and most thorough way to approach a problem. Value your self-reliance, but don't become a slave to it.

This Combination in Action
George is a take-charge guy. He was the chief salesman for a manufacturer of oil-drilling bits, a technical field with no-

nonsense customers. Those customers loved doing business with George, because they felt that George was one of *them*. He knew all about oil drilling and the special engineering of drilling bits. In fact, he knew as much as any engineer.

In twenty-five years of selling bits, George had become a legend. George relished his reputation, but he was starting to look ahead to retirement. Over the years, George had bought a lot of stock in the company he sold for, and he had more than a passing interest in the future of the firm. George decided to mentor a few good salespeople to take up where he would leave off.

Among his most promising candidates was Sally. George thought she had just about everything it takes. Like himself, she knew the business inside out. She even had an engineering degree. She knew how to give advice, and, even more important, she knew how to listen. She conveyed warmth and honesty, and she always communicated with great clarity.

There was only one problem. She was deathly afraid of soloing.

Lately, George would take her along on his sales calls, then drop back to let her make the presentation.

"You did great!" he'd say.

"Well, I couldn't have done it without you there."

Each time that George would try to send her off on her own, Sally would find some excuse to postpone. Finally, George decided to make a bold gamble. His best customer was a large drilling company that George had won over to an exclusive contract after five years of patient selling. This was his trophy account. He had lavished attention on it.

One day, George called Sally into his office.

"I'm sending you out to pitch the Simpson outfit on the new bits."

"What? They've been *your* personal customers for I don't know how many years."

"Eleven years and five months, if you want to be exact. And now it's time they met you."

"I don't know about this, George. These are *your* people."

"Look. I have complete confidence in you. You'll make the trip. Me? I'm not even coming into the office tomorrow. I need a day off. I'm not going to be near a phone or a fax or my computer. I'm going to relax, knowing that nobody knows the new bit line better than you do. You know how important this account is to me. Well, by sending you, I'm delivering the best to my customer. I'll see you Monday, after you get back."

Sally was scared, but she sold the line. On Monday, she confessed to George that it had been the hardest thing she had ever done. George just smiled. He did not confess to her just how hard it had been for *him* to take that Friday off.

DC
SELF-RELIANT AND ANALYTICAL

If, in this focus situation, your DiSC totals for both D and C are 44 or higher, you have a response pattern with high Dominance and Conscientiousness dimensions. It doesn't matter whether the D or C is higher.

You are taking an analytical approach to this situation. You probably haven't sought other people's advice. If your judgment is challenged, you'll quickly defend it, not to protect yourself but because you have carefully thought it through. You almost never act impulsively.

Value to the Group

In this situation, you may see issues others have missed or have chosen to ignore. You have been known to predict trouble *before* it happens.

DC Style

What motivates you?

- Valuing quality and accuracy
- Having time to think things through
- Working independently
- Doing your part

What discourages you?

- Sharing control over tasks you feel best qualified to handle
- Waiting for others to do their part

What is your favorite environment?

- Commitment to quality
- Time to examine issues from multiple perspectives
- Clear rules, procedures, and objectives
- High performance standards

What do you avoid?

- Impulsive actions and quick decisions
- Group analysis
- Getting advice

And that is not all you contribute. You produce work of high quality. You are a meticulous planner. And you do your share of the work.

Areas of Misunderstanding

If you are spending time thinking things through, some co-workers may think you are dragging your heels. Some people think *productivity* means *action* and have a difficult time recognizing *thought* as *work*.

Your ability to spot trouble ahead may seem like pessimism. People don't like it when someone rains on their parade.

Some people may also misinterpret your silences. You may be reserved and keep things to yourself. Others may wonder what you are thinking. Unless you speak out, they may assume all sorts of wrong ideas.

What happens when you *do* speak up? You can be blunt. You tend to stay quiet until something really bothers you. What comes out then may sound less like a comment than a complaint. Others may take you for a whiner.

Your independence and perfectionism may lead some people to think that you are hard to get along with; others may, for better or worse, think you are a maverick or a non-conformist. Well, admit it—you don't easily give in to other people's demands.

Information to Share

Plenty of your colleagues, bosses, subordinates, and customers are totally unaware of how useful planning is. In this situation, help others to see how they can benefit from your careful approach. Point out the benefits of doing things well and accurately. Be prepared to educate your colleagues, co-workers, and even your boss.

Ask questions and offer advice at the *beginning* of a project and then throughout the process. Don't wait until a crisis compels you to complain.

You *do* think things through, so you have good reason to believe that your course of action is right. But push yourself to check in with others, too.

Because you are so self-directed, it may not occur to you to ask for help. It's not that you stubbornly refuse help. You just don't think to ask. You might try two variations on your usual approach:

- Ask for help now and then. Accept it gracefully.
- Encourage others to ask for your opinions. Try to arrange discussions about how you can best help the group.

What to Look Out For

People who respond to situations with a strong DC pattern are often experts in a field. They may be highly trained, educated, or experienced. If this is you, you may feel that others know much less than you do, so it's better to work alone. Certainly, many of your skills are best applied in intense, demanding, high-quality, *solo* tasks. By all means, seize opportunities to work alone. However, many projects will involve others. You may find it frustrating to share control with colleagues who lack your skills, experience, or commitment to quality. You may also feel rushed if they don't want to devote enough time to careful planning. Impulsive actions make you mad, especially if you think they will harm your well-laid plans.

Don't let your ability to foresee problems prompt you to swat down new ideas like so many flies. It makes no sense to race down the wrong road, but it is also important to foster new ideas, encourage risk-taking, and let people make mistakes. Try softening the blow by beginning with a positive remark, followed by your doubts: "That's a really intriguing idea, George. What about the turnaround time? I see it as a minimum of sixty days. Couldn't that present a problem in this market?" Note that, by framing your doubts in the form of a question rather than a declarative statement, you empower the other person to respond. Maybe he really does have a solution. Or maybe the question will prompt someone else to come up with a solution.

Getting Unstuck

Situation: You exploded at a meeting.

Possibility: You probably have had concerns for some time, but you have kept them bottled up. Make an effort to ask questions and offer advice at the beginning of and throughout the process, not just at critical points.

Situation: You pointed out a problem, and the whole discussion ended.

Possibility: When you bring up a problem, try asking a question rather than making a statement. "How will we cope with such and such?" is easier to take than "This will never work because of such and such." While a statement tends to close the discussion, a question tends to open the discussion up so new ideas and solutions can emerge.

Situation: You know your plan is right.

Possibility: Still, check in with others and bring them on board.

Your Bottom Line

You are demanding and analytical. You save the group from taking wrong turns. You are at your very best when you work alone, producing excellent results over and over.

This Combination in Action

Alexis is the communications specialist for a regional bank. To keep in touch with all the branches, the organization sends a weekly electronic newsletter, and writing and producing it are among her main responsibilities.

Alexis responds to this challenge in a DC way, and it's a good thing she does. She draws on her C side to keep all the details under control. Week after week, the newsletter comes in on schedule. Without her D side, though, she'd never be able to push other staff members to get their stories in on time. She makes decisions quickly, day after day, while still keeping quality high.

SI
SUPPORTIVE AND FLEXIBLE

If your scores for Supportiveness and Influence are 44 or above, and if S is the same or higher than I, you have the SI response pattern in the situation on which you have focused. If, however, your S score is lower than your I score, read the next profile.

If you have a SI response pattern, you value the relationships that are part of this situation. You look hard for ways to help other people. It is very important to you that the members of your work group cooperate and work well together—especially that *you* get along well with others. You want harmony so much that you are flexible and adjust to changing demands. You look for opportunities to demonstrate that others can depend on you.

Value to the Group

Your value to the group is simply that *you value the group.*

SI Style

What motivates you?

- Positive teamwork
- Serving others
- Building good relationships
- Others depending on you

What discourages you?

- Isolated projects
- Competition
- Tension or hostility

What is your favorite environment?

- Value placed on collaboration and harmony
- Tactful and respectful communication

What do you avoid?

- Being the center of attention
- Confrontations and tense situations
- Saying no, even when it is in your best interest

You like to fit in and get along with others. Teamwork is highly rewarding for you.

You are friendly and easygoing, but not concerned about being popular. You focus on what others need and promote what you believe will make them happy. Your goal is "customer satisfaction," whether your customer is a client, colleague, or boss.

The people you work with appreciate your accommodating ways, your flexibility, and your support.

Areas of Misunderstanding

Because you are easygoing, calm, and collected, people may think you can handle *anything*. While your flexibility does get you through many difficult situations, it's tough on you when people play hardball. Similarly, you may not weather big changes as well as other people think; while you're willing to be flexible, you may be troubled by the tension that often surrounds upheavals.

Your desire to avoid conflict may lead you to turn away from confrontation. If you do, people may either take advantage of you or think you lack backbone.

Information to Share

Consider why conflict is tough for you. You are upset not by the substance of the conflict, but by the emotions attached to it. You don't want to make the other person unhappy or angry. The issues—"I think the coffee machine should be in the hall" versus "I think it should be in the break room"— become secondary to the emotions involved. Instead of avoiding the conflict, try focusing on issues and facts. Tally up the pros and cons of putting the coffee machine in the hall versus the break room. Focus on the location of the coffee machine, not on who's mad at whom.

You are generous with your support. Just be sure that

you also speak up for *your* interests now and again, or that generosity will be taken for granted and people may take advantage of you.

Your calm appearance may well lead others to believe you can handle absolutely anything. Take the time to assess your stress levels and what you must do to take care of your own needs. Just because others think there is no limit to the amount of stress you can endure doesn't mean you have to believe them.

You might lightheartedly point out to your colleagues that, while you are never one to complain, you aren't *always* happy. The next time someone tells you that you're "so easy to get along with," smile and say, "Well, I have my off days too!"

You don't like uncomfortable situations, especially situations full of conflict. Yet you are more likely to put up with such situations than to talk about them, let alone complain about them. Try not to hold back so much. It may be easier if you ask permission before expressing your concerns: "Pete, I know this is going to be your project, and I know it will be just great. But do you mind if I put my two cents in?" Or: "Mary, may I make a suggestion about the Jones account?"

What to Look Out For

You really *can't* please all of the people all of the time. Even if you could, you'd leave much unsaid. Watch out that you don't withhold important information that might displease someone or dampen the group's enthusiasm. If you let a problem slide, you may avoid a minor conflict now but set up a major one down the road.

Sometimes, the best solution to a problem won't make everyone happy. Sometimes, you'll have to say no, for the good of the group.

What if you don't speak up about a problem you see? Someone else will, right? Maybe. What happens if everyone else keeps quiet, too?

Getting Unstuck

Situation: You see a problem, but you don't speak up.
Possibility: Your flexibility can be valuable in times of change, but it isn't wise to support a decision you think is not in the best interests of the group or project.

Situation: Someone is taking advantage of you.
Possibility: You are generous in your support of others, but you need to speak up for yourself, too.

Situation: You are under too much stress.
Possibility: Because you appear calm, others may think you can handle anything. Be aware of your sources of stress and take care of yourself.

Your Bottom Line

Look for ways you can help others in this situation. Your generous support will be very good for them and highly rewarding for you.

This Combination in Action

John is a customer-service representative for a large mail-order firm. He has taken the DiSC instrument a number of times, each time focusing on a customer-service issue. Each time he has emerged with an SI response pattern.

His customer-service mantra is, "Never say no."

A trainer once asked him, "John, do you mean you can always give customers what they want? You really never have to say no? Must be some company you work for."

"Well," John answered, "it's not always that easy. But I

approach each customer-service call by telling myself that 'no' isn't an option. That way, I avoid a knee-jerk no. For me, with my high SI, saying no is hard. But I've learned that just because you can't give the customer exactly what he asks for, you don't have to say no.

"Let's say a customer calls to change her order. I check on the computer, and I find that the order has already been shipped. Now, do I tell the customer that it's too late to change her order? No. Instead, I begin by reporting the facts:

"'Ms. Smith, that order was shipped out two days ago. What I can do is take your order for the other item now and send it out with a return label enclosed. Hold on to the original order, don't unpack it, and when the new item arrives, just slap the return label on the original order and send it on back.'

"Basically, I say no without ever having to say no. That is, I skip over the no part and go directly to an alternative. It's easier for me, and a lot more satisfying to the customer, to say what I can do rather than what I can't.'"

IS
ENCOURAGING AND COOPERATIVE

If you have high scores for Influence and Supportiveness—both 44 or above—but with I higher than S, you have an IS response pattern in this situation.

You focus on building relationships that will benefit you. You help yourself by helping others.

The IS response pattern frequently emerges in situations calling for leadership. Leaders responding with an IS pattern are often effective mentors, encouraging others to develop and grow.

IS Style

What motivates you?

▷ Working on a team
▷ Leading or influencing a group
▷ Growing and learning
▷ Developing useful relationships

What discourages you?

▷ Lack of visibility or recognition
▷ Being burdened with other people's feelings or problems

What is your favorite environment?

▷ Secure and open
▷ Pleasant and trusting
▷ Expression of rewards and appreciation

What do you avoid?

▷ Dependent people
▷ Arguing

Value to the Group

You love leading. You lead by example, and you lead by encouraging others to develop their abilities. Others may seek your coaching.

You speak up for yourself, and you are often happy to speak up for others as well. Your friendly manner inspires confidence and trust. No wonder you are often asked to be a spokesperson for the group.

You shine when you're the center of attention, though you don't grab the spotlight if it might cause trouble.

In your focus situation, you very much want to keep things pleasant. You are trying to be the center of calm. You don't throw fuel on the fire. Instead, you stay calm and let others lead you and the group toward a solution. Sometimes you try to build understanding within the group by voicing people's concerns. If tempers flare, your calming, comfortable manner may hold the group together so it can keep working toward a solution.

Areas of Misunderstanding

You appear so friendly and cooperative that people feel comfortable asking you for advice. This is fine with you up to a point, but you don't want to be burdened by other people's problems. While you have the potential to be a mentor or coach, you don't want to act as personal counselor or therapist. You care about people's feelings, but you don't want to spend too much time contemplating them or worrying about them.

Similarly, you value work relationships as *work* relationships and as opportunities to exercise and expand your influence, but you are not comfortable when people bring their personal problems to work.

You can be an effective spokesperson for your position

as well as the position of others. However, because you do not enjoy debating, you speak out only on safe issues, those not likely to lead to an argument. Sometimes this is wise, but people who expect you to speak up may feel you've let them down. You may be perceived as someone who can't be counted on. Your loyalty may be doubted even. The truth is just that you do not like conflict.

This is unfair, of course, because you never intended to proclaim yourself anyone's champion, but you need to be aware of this danger zone.

Information to Share

A fuzzy line separates the roles of coach and counselor. It is up to you to clarify where the line is for you. Follow your inclination to be generous with advice and guidance in a professional context, but don't accept openings to discuss personal and family matters. If you are a mentor or manager, there are times when you'll have to deal with personal issues, but don't go there any more than necessary.

How can you avoid misunderstandings about how far you're prepared to go in advocating for someone or for your group? Don't get into the situation in the first place. Resist the temptation to speak out on every issue, or you'll find yourself saddled with ones you don't want.

While you usually aren't shy about telling others what you need, you may well hold back if you think you'll trigger a dispute. In situations where differences of opinion are likely to surface, it may be a good idea to let others know that you don't like to argue. "One problem I have," you might say, "is making unpopular decisions. But I know that such decisions are sometimes necessary. Can I count on your support?"

What to Look Out For

Make certain that people understand that you are willing to be a coach and mentor, but not a therapist. Demonstrate that you are selective about fighting battles. Resist the temptation to speak up about everything that comes your way. Make certain that when you do choose to speak out, you are willing to go all the way and not drop out when things get sticky. Understand that you can be a good friend but that, in a work context, the friendship you offer others may be limited.

Getting Unstuck

Situation: Someone thinks you are a personal therapist.

Possibilities: You don't want to come across as insensitive or self-centered, but you don't want to take on this person's problems. One possibility is to make it clear that you're happy to be a mentor, but you don't want to get into the personal stuff. Another possibility is to take a little time to listen. If you have advice to give, fine. If not, this really is not *your* problem or *your* responsibility. You have already been helpful just by listening.

Situation: You stopped pushing for an idea when you met resistance, and now others think you let them down.

Possibility: Pick your next battle more carefully, making sure you're willing to go the distance.

Your Bottom Line

You find it easy and natural to gather a group around you. The fact is, though, you may be more interested in assembling such a group than you are in serving its needs. There is a danger that others may feel let down, disillusioned, disappointed.

You can be a gifted mentor, but again, set limits on the kinds of help you are willing to give.

Outgoing, pleasant, and cooperative, you bring much positive energy to the situation. Just try not to lead people to expect help you are unwilling to deliver.

This Combination in Action

Sometimes it is a great gift to remind a group what it is all about. This is a classic IS response.

Phil was a salesman for a small southeastern software firm that had just had a rude awakening. The company was collecting a steady flow of revenue from a line of customized accounting packages. Everyone had been excited, however, about a new Internet-related product, which would be a departure for the company but looked very promising. A good deal of time, energy, and cash had been put into developing the product when, months before the scheduled launch, another company burst onto the market with a cheaper and better version of what was in the works.

Phil walked into a meeting at which the president of the firm was pulling the plug on the project. The meeting was disintegrating into bickering and blaming.

Phil had no desire to join in, but he was thinking about the situation differently. Though he felt uncomfortable, he chose to speak up.

"There's no way I'm going to get up here and cheerlead. This is a lousy thing that's happened, and I, for one, was really looking forward to selling the hell out of the product.

"But it's not happening now, so let's put it aside and get back to what we've been doing very well for five years. Nobody is offering the kind of customized solutions we offer at the price we offer them. This has always been our goal. The new direction didn't pan out. So be it. We're still awfully good at what we do. Let's remember that.

"I was excited about selling the new product. But I'm even more excited about selling the Thompson account tomorrow on a new version of the package they've been using. We'll sell them twenty additional installations. And the next day, I'll be excited about selling the next account.

"Let's take our lumps and then remember what we do best and just keep on doing it—better and better."

Did everyone at the postmortem meeting suddenly get happy? Of course not. But they went home at the end of the day, and they all came back the next day, and they went to work—together.

IC
TACTFUL AND OBSERVANT

An IC response to the situation depends on whether you are focusing on people or tasks. When you relate to *people,* you are confident, sensitive, and tactful. When you turn to *tasks,* you are intensely observant and attentive to details.

What do these reactions have in common? Reliability. Your organization can count on you, whether the situation calls for people skills or high-quality results.

Value to the Group
You get along well with others. Your flexibility is especially valuable. You don't complain; you contribute. And when the group needs high-quality results, it can count on you to meet the highest standards. The combination makes you an MVP on any team.

Areas of Misunderstanding
When you are focusing intensely on a task, others may think you are tuning them out, particularly if they've usually seen your "people side." It's true that your focus narrows when you're on task, but not because you no longer care about others.

IC Style

What motivates you?

▷ A mixture of working independently and working with others

▷ Accuracy and quality are important

What discourages you?

▷ Lack of acknowledgment of your good work

▷ No opportunity to work on independent projects

▷ Being taken advantage of

▷ Tolerance of sloppy work

What is your favorite environment?

▷ Loyalty to other employees and to the organization

▷ Value placed on high standards and integrity

▷ Expressions of recognition and appreciation

▷ Effective and flexible teams

What do you avoid?

▷ Risks

▷ Acting without prior analysis

▷ Unexpected changes

▷ Arguments

People also misunderstand your approach to change. You don't like risks, and you believe in analyzing a situation before taking action, but you're more open to new ideas than others may think. You are not opposed to trying new ideas, and while you may not initiate change, you generally adapt well to it. Your role in innovation is often to spot good ideas and promote them to the group. While the initiators often get the credit, it is advancers like you who move ideas forward. Others may not give you enough credit for your contribution.

Cheerful and reliable, you may seem content with or without praise, but positive feedback is important to you. Although you bring to the group an abundance of warmth and goodwill, your enthusiasm may fade if you don't receive credit when due, though you are not one to fish for compliments.

Information to Share

When you accomplish something of which you are proud, *ask* for feedback. You don't have to pump your colleagues for compliments, but give them openings. Everybody is refreshed and encouraged by praise.

Even if you are quite dissatisfied with a situation, you will probably try to stick it out in the hope that it will get better. It is not likely that you will speak up. Besides, you don't want to start an argument.

Sometimes, it is true, little benefit can be gained by complaining. Some situations cannot be easily changed. It may seem that the best strategy is to wait it out. This approach has one major problem: the *meantime*. For, in the *meantime*, you may be pushed around and taken advantage of. Despite your unhappiness, you are likely to remain loyal and hard-working, even if others aren't doing their parts. Is there an alternative to standing by until something changes?

Maybe. Consider using your warmth and enthusiasm for others to help you express your own ideas and insights, not only for your own good, but for that of the group. Sometimes, it's worth it to be proactive.

What to Look Out For

Try to avoid being pigeonholed as either a "people person" or a "task person." Just because you work well alone, concentrating on details, doesn't mean that you cannot also perform well with customers, investors, or the general public. Confident and outgoing, you should not live out all of your professional life in the back office.

On the other hand, your demonstrated people skills may prompt supervisors and others to assign you exclusively to group tasks and people-focused work. The problem is that you probably also want time to work independently.

Your ideal position will allow both time to work alone as well as plenty of contact with other people. Versatility like this is unusual, so it is too often overlooked and wasted.

Getting Unstuck

Situation: Your job doesn't make good use of your people skills.

Possibilities: The most effective way to alert your colleagues and co-workers to the range of your capabilities is to demonstrate them. If you have a technical specialty or special knowledge, consider offering a workshop or informal lunchtime presentation. Or take on the company's annual charity drive. Show how well you relate to human beings as well as tasks.

Situation: You're toughing it out until things get better.

Possibility: Use your warmth and enthusiasm to help you express your own ideas and insights for your own good and the good of the group.

Your Bottom Line

While you are committed to excellence, you don't intimidate or alienate others. You are highly adaptable. This makes working with you easy and rewarding. Just remember that even a flexible stick can snap if it is pushed too hard, too fast, or too often.

This Combination in Action

Here is a story with a happy ending.

Elias was always interested in electronics. When he was a boy, he tinkered with radio sets. After high school, he went to a technical school. He started working for an office machine company as a field technical representative, traveling on-site to repair copy machines and other equipment.

His supervisors always received positive comments on Elias's work. Frequently, clients would remark that he was friendly and easy to talk to. "Not a lot of technical people are like that," one client said.

Elias was pleased that his work was appreciated, but as the years on the job added up, he became aware that his career wasn't giving him everything he wanted. He spoke to his boss, who offered him a promotion to a middle-level management position. Elias knew that a promotion was the road to success, yet he knew he would miss working hands-on with the machines. Getting bumped up to a supervisory position would mean the end of that.

Elias's boss was puzzled by his hesitation. He asked Elias just what it was that he wanted.

"Oh," Elias said, "I guess I just want too much. I really enjoy tackling the technical problems—fixing things that don't work. But I also miss dealing with people. To tell you the truth, the service calls I enjoy most are those that require explaining how something works. I like making these machines understandable to people. Those big color printers can be pretty complicated for some users, and I enjoy setting it all out in front of them."

Elias's boss had an idea. He made some phone calls and, a few days later, called Elias back into his office.

"How would you like to train field representatives? It is a teaching and coaching role that will also require you to work hands-on, side by side with your students—as well as with our engineers, as they bring out new models."

Elias had found his dream job.

SC
RESPECTFUL AND ACCURATE

If your totals for S and C equal or exceed 44, in this situation you are careful with people, and you are careful with tasks. You are supportive, respectful, and very much concerned that you never be the source of problems or conflict. The people you work with, even your bosses, probably come to you from time to time in search of a sympathetic ear. You are very willing to listen, empathize, and offer thoughtful counsel.

This kind of respectful support is important to your group, although, like the foundation of a great building, it lies below the surface. That's okay with you. You do not want to be the center of attention.

Value to the Group

You want to provide a stable foundation for the group's activities, so you do what you can to encourage:

- clear objectives and goals
- defined standards and expectations
- time for planning and analysis

SC Style

What motivates you?

➤ Ample time to analyze the issues
➤ Consideration for people's time and concerns
➤ Clear, meaningful, specific instructions

What discourages you?

➤ Rush assignments
➤ Lack of concern for the impact of tasks on people
➤ Unclear direction

What is your favorite environment?

➤ Stable
➤ Clear goals and objectives
➤ Clearly defined expectations and standards

What do you avoid?

➤ Being the center of attention
➤ Having to verbalize thoughts and feelings
➤ Crash projects
➤ Quick decisions
➤ Surprises

Conversely, you discourage:

- rushed assignments
- impulsive action
- lack of concern for how something may affect people
- unclear directions
- loosely defined job descriptions or performance standards
- group hysteria

The stability you bring to a group also extends to relationships. You avoid conflict—and even help others avoid it. Because you want to understand the issues involved in conflict, you may discover ways to prevent or solve the problem. You may intervene—in a subtle, nonthreatening way, of course.

Areas of Misunderstanding

Quiet, content to stay well outside of the limelight, you can be underappreciated. As valuable as your quiet, analytical ways can be, they mean nothing to the group if you never speak up. Your quiet ways may lead others to underestimate you and what you know. People may assume you don't speak up because you have little to say, and they won't ask for your ideas, even when they would be very useful.

Information to Share

You can benefit a great deal by telling others about yourself. Overcoming your natural inclination to remain silent will probably take some effort; but it can be worth it.

Let others know that you don't like short deadlines and are not at your best when you are rushed to make decisions. Try to discuss the amount of time you'll need to make sure that your work is done to your satisfaction and to the satisfaction of the group.

At the start of a project, suggest that there be a discussion of the objectives, goals, progress markers, and criteria for evaluation. You'll want to know clearly how you fit into a particular project. Generally, the more information you obtain and you share, both early in a project and throughout its course, the better and more confident you will feel about the work.

Finally, be aware that no one can read your mind. Others may mistake your quiet ways for lack of knowledge, and this not only may inhibit your career, but will deprive the group of what you have to offer. Make the extra effort to speak out.

What to Look Out For

Complete accuracy is an asset when time is adequate, but it can cause problems when time is short and a certain degree of error or risk is acceptable. The best can be the enemy of the good. While waiting to achieve perfection, your company can lose out on an opportunity. You can also lose the support of people who feel that action is needed now.

When the time is available, advocate for taking it, since thinking things through often yields valuable insights and solutions. When time is short and a decision is needed, draw on your experience. Though you don't have the time you want to examine the present problem or crisis, you may be able to draw parallels to a similar situation in the past. You thought things through *then*—use those insights *now*. Relying on your experience should help minimize the risks of taking action.

Getting Unstuck

Situation: There are too many unknowns in your project.
Possibility: Consider preparing a simple worksheet for a launch meeting at the start of every project. Include on the

worksheet blanks for the principal requirements of the project: specifications, costs, deadlines, schedules, evaluation sessions, and so on. Pass the sheets around at the meeting. Filling in the blanks will help focus the meeting and will create a written record of the parameters of the project.

Situation: There's no time for a complete analysis of the problem.
Possibility: Accept that some risk is okay when time is short and a decision has to be made. Draw on your past experience, and contribute your insights and solutions.

Situation: Nobody asked for your opinion.
Possibility: If you think you can help, offer your ideas—even if you haven't been asked.

Your Bottom Line

While you see yourself as quiet, others may come to see you as an important source of solutions. "Still waters run deep" describes you. While others spin their wheels, you stand by, paying close attention and quietly analyzing the issues. You often ground the group.

Your need for clarity and certainty can be an asset for your organization. When time is short, however, or in a rapidly changing situation, it can lead to frustration—both for you and for others. Don't give up. Try to generate thought and discussion about mutual goals, objectives, and purpose. Even when quick movement is required, it is still important to move in the right direction, and your insightful caution may help the group do just that. However, complete accuracy is not always critical. When time is limited, it is necessary to accept a degree of risk. Accept that you will feel some stress and anxiety, but that sometimes a decision simply has to be made.

This Combination in Action

A management consultant told me about her work for a Silicon Valley firm that had pulled together a team to create a human-resources software program.

"When I entered the picture," she said, "the team, working on an eighteen-month deadline, was already nine months into the schedule without producing a thing. They were supposed to be piloting an initial software piece at a carefully chosen location. At this point, however, they couldn't decide on the software, and they couldn't decide on the location.

"Management called me in to do conflict resolution. One of my first steps was to have team members complete the DiSC instrument. There were nineteen people on the team. Eighteen were high Ds or high-D combinations, and one was an SC combination.

"High-D people can be pretty forceful in their conversation. Listening to them, you'd think they were always arguing, but actually they were just forceful.

"During the course of the first day of our conflict-resolution work, the SC woman left the room several times, then would come back. That first day ended, and the next day we began talking about one of the challenges we had discovered: the fact that each person wanted only his or her ideas included in the final version of the software and insisted on his or her nominee for test location. Nobody would yield an inch. And this is what had been happening for the past nine months.

"Well, that second day of conflict resolution started going the same way. Each person wanted his or her own idea accepted, and only that idea.

"Suddenly, the woman who had shown an SC combination stood up. It actually took a couple of moments for the rest of the team to acknowledge that there she was, standing.

"When it was clear that she had their attention, she quietly said—and she was shaking— 'Have you noticed that I come to these meetings, and I say very little? I was put on this team because I'm a systems person. I understand the current systems better than anyone. But you never ask me for my input. You never listen to me when I try to say something. Did any of you ever notice that during meetings I leave every once in awhile?' A few had noticed. Many hadn't.

"'When I leave the room, it's because I can't stand the tension. I can't stand the level of confrontation. Yesterday, I left the room twice, and I went to the bathroom, and I threw up.

"'Well, last night, I made a decision. And the decision was, I'm either on the team or I'm not. I wrote down what I need for me to be on the team. This is what has to happen for me. If it can't happen, I don't want to be on this team anymore, because I can't put up with this.

"'I want to be acknowledged, listened to, included. I don't want to fight to get the floor. If my contribution can't be made in a way that's comfortable for me, I don't want to be here anymore.'

"In a very dramatic fashion, then, the team members suddenly saw how their behavior impacted other people. In that moment, they began to understand why they never got anywhere. They understood the consequences of the it's-my-way-or-the-highway approach. Equally important, they also understood that a very valuable team member wasn't being allowed to contribute. It was not because anybody was maliciously trying to exclude her. It was because her style was different from everyone else's on the team.

"With this new understanding, everyone worked to flex, to adapt. The result? The woman did stay on the team, and the team did get back on track. They didn't pull off a miracle in the nine months they had left. The project was delayed, but it did happen, and disaster was averted."

DIS
COMFORTABLE AND ENGAGED

If, in the situation you have chosen to focus on, your totals for the D, I, *and* S styles are each 44 or higher, your response pattern combines strong elements of the Dominance, Influence, and Supportiveness dimensions.

If you are responding with a DIS pattern, you are feeling comfortable and well satisfied in that particular situation. You are glad that the situation is giving you opportunities to be friendly and helpful—and that others are appreciating your support.

In this situation, you are taking action! If this makes you the center of attention, that's fine with you. You are always willing to take on a leadership role.

You are strongly motivated by situations in which you can work with and encourage a group. You want to have fun, too. Most of the time, you enjoy yourself. To put it simply: You're happy!

But certain situations don't make you at all happy. For example, you have little patience for intense concentration on detail. As a "people person," you don't do your best when called on to work alone for long periods. You also don't like work environments in which your contributions are not openly appreciated or in which a lack of concern for others is clear.

Value to the Group

In this situation, your enthusiasm can get others moving. As others see the satisfaction you feel in working toward the goal, they may come to recognize and value the goal, too. All they have to do is watch you—and your high profile makes that easy.

DIS Style

What motivates you?

- A positive outlook
- Fun
- Encouraging a group
- When contributions are recognized

What discourages you?

- Detailed tasks
- Lack of concern or appreciation for people
- Little opportunity to work with others

What is your favorite environment?

- Working with others toward common goals
- Good visibility
- Enjoying yourself
- Positive attitudes
- Success is celebrated and rewarded

What do you avoid?

- Detailed, tedious projects
- Isolation
- Negativity

When the going gets tough, people may look to you for encouragement, for while your optimism isn't blind, you are good at finding the positive side of the situation. You find the fun in the work, too.

Areas of Misunderstanding

It's difficult to dislike you, but it's not impossible!

Somebody may feel jealous or resentful of your popularity. Some may not understand that your friendliness and desire to help are genuine, not just a power grab. Active and energetic as you drive toward the goal, you may be seen as pushy. However, since you're well liked and influential, people who dislike you probably won't let on. You may be resented *silently*—then someday get a knife in your back.

Another danger area is your avoidance of tedious or routine tasks. Others may feel they're being saddled with the boring jobs while you take the fun stuff.

Finally, although your optimism is extremely valuable to the group, some people may see you as a Pollyanna, someone whose optimism is habitual, unthinking, and unrealistic. They may question your judgment.

Information to Share

It is a good idea to make explicit how important you feel it is for the group to achieve its goals. Take every opportunity to tell people you are committed to realizing the *common* objectives of the group.

When it is time to divide the tasks, you might explain that details are not your forte. Ask for the tasks to which you are best suited. At the same time, volunteer for some of the more routine jobs, to show that you are willing to pitch in.

What to Look Out For

As pointed out earlier, some people may think that your helpfulness is a grab for influence or power. They may resent, undermine, or blindside you.

Beware of detailed, tedious projects requiring many hours of work in isolation. They're just not for you.

Finally, if you try to help everybody all the time, you'll probably start losing your concentration, especially if you are working long hours or with a complex, detailed problem. By trying to help everyone, you may burn out.

Getting Unstuck

Situation: You've been asked to do a stint of solo work.
Possibilities: Build some social time into your days. Take some short breaks in the coffee room or wherever people tend to gather. Schedule lunch or breakfast with colleagues. Camaraderie is very important to you. Why try to deny it? You'll return to work refreshed and ready to concentrate again.

Situation: You've excused yourself from routine tasks.
Possibilities: Take your turn, to show the rest of the group you're a fair person.

Situation: Work hasn't been much fun lately.
Possibilities: Consider that while a positive outlook is good, work is not always going to be fun. Or shake things up, and plan that overdue staff party.

Situation: You feel burned out.
Possibilities: Are you spending too much energy encouraging others? Are you spending too much on your projects? Have you rewarded yourself lately?

Your Bottom Line

Tedious solo projects may not be for you, but almost all work has some stretches you'll find boring or depressing. Draw on your deep optimism to put some positive energy back in the project—overcoming your own frustration and inspiring the group as well.

Remember that even you don't have limitless stores of optimism and energy. You can't be all things to all people all of the time. It is possible to devote too much energy to continually encouraging others.

This Combination in Action

Sally was a graduate student in history and worked part time at the state historical society. With a small staff, the society put out a modest but popular local history magazine that circulated to 7,500 readers throughout the state. The magazine was always up against its deadline, the small staff sometimes working through the night to put the issue to bed. When it came back from the printer, there was always a crunch to get it mailed. To save money, labeling was done in-house, in a back room of the historical society's building. The same computer that was used to lay out the magazine spit out 7,500 labels, arranged and sorted in the zip-code order the post office requires for bulk mailing.

Sally was an able scholar, but she was even better suited to classroom teaching. She liked to *facilitate* learning. Her favorite times when working on the magazine were the creative sessions with the other staff members—getting together to discuss what articles to publish, which ones needed further work by the authors, and consigning some to the "hopeless" bin. Sally enjoyed talking with or writing to authors, but she left to others the nitty-gritty editing tasks—correcting the grammar, checking the spelling, tracking down sources of information to ensure accuracy.

Like everyone else, though, she pitched in to slap mailing labels on the finished magazines. It was mindless work, but the camaraderie of doing the job, with people she liked, made it more than tolerable.

Then disaster struck. A hard-disk crash trashed the database used to generate the mailing labels. An old backup existed, but unfortunately it was out of date. The group members put their heads together and decided that there was nothing to do except use the old backup to print up labels and then make a lot of corrections by hand to update the database. It would be tedious, time-consuming work. Even with everyone working on it, this would be an all-nighter.

"This isn't going to be fun," the editor-in-chief remarked.

At first, Sally's heart sank. This was not the way she had planned to spend her evening. The editor's words echoed around in her head: This isn't going to be fun. The next thing she knew, Sally found herself saying, "Oh, we'll *make* it fun."

She passed the hat and collected enough cash for pizza all around.

Somebody else said, "You know, I have an old turntable at home and a stack of great sixties tunes."

"We can spare you for twenty minutes," Sally said. "Go get it!"

IDC
CONFIDENT AND DETERMINED

Your response to this situation combines strong elements of three dimensions: Influence, Dominance, and Conscientiousness.

You probably feel a strong need to take charge of this situation—and to remain in charge. You believe you know what needs to be done and just how to do it, and you feel confident that you can meet whatever challenges come your way. You are committed to whatever approach you have chosen, and you aren't about to let anything—or anyone—interfere with your plans. This does not mean, however, that you are unwilling to help others as you move toward your objectives. Quite the opposite—you feel motivated to help others along the way.

Value to the Group

You thrive on demanding projects. Not only do you want to meet the challenges, but you want to help others meet the challenges, too. Your leadership often includes identifying and clarifying the goal and what it will take to reach it. Similarly, you are often the first to spot the need for a change and can lead the way through the transition.

The Dominance and Influence dimensions draw your attention to the big picture, but your strong Conscientiousness dimension draws your attention to the important details. People who are responding with an IDC pattern not only assess and articulate the big issues, but handle the bits and pieces.

Highly tuned in to what's going on around you and strong in your opinions, you usually speak with confidence, energy, and directness. A forceful, outspoken person with a firm grasp on the realities of the situation is always valuable to a group.

Areas of Misunderstanding

You come on strong. Your confidence, determination, and plain talk may be seen as arrogance, abrasiveness, or lack of caring.

IDC Style

What motivates you?

- Being in charge
- Taking on new challenges
- Developing solutions

What discourages you?

- Not having authority
- Not dealing openly with issues
- Working with people who aren't concerned about quality or doing things right

What is your favorite environment?

- Demanding projects
- Helping others achieve clearly articulated goals

What do you avoid?

- Not thinking things through
- People who are not willing to push forward
- Questioning of your ideas or judgment

Information to Share

Okay, you come on strong. Own up to it: "Sometimes I think I put things a little too strongly. It's nothing personal—just the way I approach people, I guess." Let people know that this is just your style in some situations. They may understand you, even like you, a little more.

You'll also seem less arrogant if you make it clear that you want to create a work environment that is rewarding and enjoyable for everyone involved. Also emphasize your commitment to excellence and quality.

Take the time to listen to others and to discuss their ideas.

What to Look Out For

You like to move quickly. In many situations, this is a good thing, but consider taking more time when circumstances allow. The additional time can pay off:

- If you take more time when making a decision, you are more likely to be tolerant and accepting of opinions different from your own.
- By taking some time alone, you may be able to determine more fully what needs to be done, as well as how to do it.
- The added time makes it easier to communicate your ideas to others and to invite their analysis.
- More time can also allow others who don't move as fast as you do to come on board.

Getting Unstuck

Situation: You are leading, but no one is following.

Possibility: Not everyone can move toward change and goals as quickly as you. Look behind you from time to time, and bring the slow ones on board.

Situation: People with alternative points of view are slowing you down.

Possibility: Try not to think of people as obstacles, but as potential supporters. Just by listening to them, you may make some allies.

Situation: People don't listen to you.

Possibility: Honesty is good, but it can make people uncomfortable. Try clearing the way by asking for permission before you speak. Ask, "Would you like to hear my thoughts on this?" or "May I share something with you about this matter?"

Your Bottom Line

You keep sight of the ultimate goals, while not overlooking the myriad details important to achieving them. This rare dual perspective is of inestimable value to your organization, particularly when projects are long or complex. Team members can look to you both for the big picture and for quality control.

This Combination in Action

Molly liked being in charge. She received high marks from her boss for what he called her "strong leadership" of the customer-support department.

"Strong leadership." Molly loved the sound of that phrase. She was willing to train her staff and even to mentor those who seemed particularly promising. However, there was also a streak in her that was all about getting things done.

Don't explain. Don't discuss. Just give the orders.

One day, Molly wrote a memo to her staff on how to handle returns of malfunctioning merchandise. Customers usually wanted the company to replace the item, not repair it, yet often a simple repair could put things right. The question was, How do you get customers to accept—happily—repair rather than replacement?

Molly's memo instructed her customer-support staff to explain to customers that "items sent for factory repair are thoroughly inspected and tested, so that we know they will function flawlessly. Repaired items are actually subjected to more quality testing than replacement items."

Testing was an important point to make to customers, and Molly was eager to ensure that all the customer-support reps would deliver the message with sincere conviction. She thought about this issue: How can I get my staff to get this message across so that our customers will feel satisfied?

Then the answer occurred to her.

To get her *customers* to buy into the message, she first had to get her *own staff* to buy into it.

Couldn't she just issue the memo and direct the staff to deliver her words with conviction?

Well, of course she could do that. But Molly understood that much as she would like to take the simple, direct route of telling everyone what to say and how to say it, she would get the support she needed only if she allowed her staff input into the plan. Molly put the memo aside and called a staff meeting. She asked the reps to brainstorm on the topic of selling to customers the idea of repair versus replacement.

As it turned out, the statement everyone finally agreed on was much the same statement Molly had formulated in the first place. But a critical difference wasn't reflected in the words on paper. The difference was that, now, the words belonged to everyone who had to use them, not just to a strong-willed boss. The process had taken time certainly, and Molly wasn't the most patient person in the world, but giving everyone an ownership stake in this important customer-support message had been worth it.

With high D, S, and C, your response to the situation is reflecting strong Dominance, Supportiveness, and Conscientiousness dimensions.

You probably find the focus situation challenging, and you feel that circumstances should be improved or corrected. Certainly, you are not content with things the way they are, and you hope to change them. On the positive side, you've been inspired to take responsibility for seeing that things are done well and that goals are met. You welcome the chance to use all of your skills and experience, and you are willing to be held personally responsible for the results.

While you may feel inspired by situations others find difficult, you find discouraging situations in which the goals are undefined, unclear, or contradictory; details are downplayed, overlooked, or handled sloppily; or high quality is not considered important or is not appreciated.

If you are taking up a challenge in this situation, you probably feel that the first step is to establish ground rules and procedures—based on objective standards, not on someone's mood or whim. This is not to say that you think rules are more important than people. Consideration for other people's needs and efforts is very important to you.

Value to the Group

For you, "doing things well" means making things run smoothly and successfully not just for you, but for everyone.

You are the person to whom others turn when details are important—when error cannot be tolerated. Others may see you as an expert or veteran, even if you are fairly new to the job. You learn from experience quickly and efficiently and

DSC Style

What motivates you?

- Improving situations and achieving goals
- Using your skills and experience
- Being personally accountable

What discourages you?

- Unclear goals
- Lack of attention to detail
- Ignoring quality

What is your favorite environment?

- Clear rules and processes
- Clearly communicated expectations
- Emphasis on doing the job well

What do you avoid?

- Poorly defined expectations and responsibilities for yourself and others
- Being left out of key decisions
- People who don't carry their share of the workload
- Conflict

find it natural to apply your knowledge to new situations.

Your strong need for clearly and objectively defined goals and rules can help your group move toward concrete results. You may motivate the group to evaluate and perhaps modify its aims and procedures.

While you demand carefulness and precision from yourself and others in the group, the high level of Supportiveness in your response usually means that you are no slave to the rules. You consider the needs and feelings of others.

Areas of Misunderstanding

Although Supportiveness is an important aspect of your behavior in this situation, sometimes you may be paying more attention to rules, to procedures, and to how well things are done than to how others feel about the rules, the procedures, or the issues involved. Even if this isn't actually the case, others may, from time to time, *think* that you feel this way. It is possible, then, that others may see only your focus on tasks and fail to see your genuine concern for people. This can put distance between you and the group.

Information to Share

The most vital information you can share is how important it is for you—and for the group—to agree on clear goals and clear procedures.

In this situation, you are probably assuming a good deal of responsibility. In fact, you may be feeling that the burden is falling on you alone. Make it clear that you are very willing to assume responsibility but that you need to know what's expected of you and what role you are to play. Invite frequent and frank feedback.

While you aren't reluctant to take on responsibility, you

do not necessarily want a leadership role in this situation. Nevertheless, you would like to take part in making key decisions. Let people know that you want to be kept in the loop.

What to Look Out For

In some situations, you may take too much of the responsibility on yourself. You may do this because you think you are the best person for the job. You may do it because you want to avoid conflicts that can arise when people who work together don't agree on how to handle the details. You may become so focused on doing a project yourself that you forget to enlist the support of others. Not only might this endanger the project, but it can lead others to overlook or ignore you. You may not be included when important decisions are made. Also, you may start to resent that others aren't doing their share of the work.

Your ability to focus intensely on problems is valuable, but don't let it overpower your S dimension. Let others in on what you are doing. Support them, and look for their support of you and your work. Take the time to think about and to talk about the ways you could use some help. This not only will keep you from taking on a crushing amount of the work, but it will also build community. Inclusiveness will help create a climate of mutual supportiveness rather than mutual resentment.

You may feel that you are perfectly capable of doing the job on your own. Well, you probably are. Perhaps the support you need is something different than help with day-to-day tasks. Support can also take the form of feedback, recognition, and encouragement. Your performance standards and sense of responsibility are so high that you tend to be critical of yourself. Others can put your performance into perspective. You put yourself under a lot of stress, and they can take some of it off.

Getting Unstuck

Situation: You feel like a beast of burden.
Possibility: Let others know what you need. Practice saying no.

Situation: You're hardest on yourself.
Possibility: Listen to the feedback of others to gain perspective and ease your stress.

Situation: Other people don't want to take the time to define the parameters and goals of new projects.
Possibility: When you are defining the rules, procedures, and goals at the beginning of a project, instead of saying, "What procedures are we going to follow?" or "Let's lay down some ground rules," try pointing out the value of this step for everyone: "It will make the work easier and faster for all of us if we set up some procedures we can all agree on." Use words like "we," "us," and "our." You'll convey that you don't think that the rules are more important than the people they are supposed to serve.

Your Bottom Line

Your objective, methodical, and disciplined approach to tasks can bring order and stability to an uncertain or risky situation. While others may be overwhelmed by the magnitude of a project, you can help break it down into manageable steps so the group can move rationally toward a well-defined goal. Moreover, you are unlikely to overlook the important details that can make the difference between a successful outcome and a disappointing one.

The DSC response pattern combines attention to detail and a commitment to excellence with a high regard for the needs and effort of others, as well as a desire and ability to speak up and make your observations known. Just don't become so intensely focused on solo work that you remove yourself from the team or alienate others.

This Combination in Action

Patti started as a sales associate with a department store in the spring. By fall, it was clear to the manager of the women's sportswear department that Patti was a real find. Customers liked her, but her flair for retailing was most evident in the way she could make just the right small adjustments to a merchandise display to make it more effective.

The manager decided that Patti was ready for more responsibility. Sales of accessories had not been keeping pace with other items in the department, so the manager called Patti over to the accessories counter.

"We're not moving this merchandise as well as we should. I need your help. How would you like to try your hand at rearranging the counter? Set it up to *sell.*"

Patti seized the opportunity.

"What am I allowed to do with the counter? What are the rules?"

"No rules," the manager said. "Just use the counter space more effectively than it's being used now. Well, one rule: I don't want this counter down for more than a day."

Patti set to work with a passion.

She radically rearranged the merchandise, adjusting this, moving that, then standing back for a look.

It was exciting work, but, somehow, the counter never looked quite right to Patti.

"How's it going?" co-workers asked.

"Oh, just fine," Patti answered each time.

But she was getting worried, and, as the day drew to a close, the manager began to wonder if she had made a mistake. What was taking so long? With Patti busy working on the display, customers were reluctant to browse. She couldn't afford a second day of downtime for the counter. By four in the afternoon, the manager was about to approach Patti with a directive to wrap it up. But she held back as she watched a customer approach the counter.

"Excuse me," the customer said.

"Yes?" Patti looked up. She realized that her voice betrayed her irritation at having been interrupted in her work. So she went on to offer, "How may I help you?"

"I just wanted to say that this is a perfectly lovely display."

Patti paused. Then, *"Really?"* she said, in some astonishment.

"Why, yes. Very pretty." And the customer walked on.

The manager, having witnessed the exchange, saw that the time was right to make her move. "Patti," she said, "the counter is finished. Don't you think it looks great?"

"Well, that lady sure liked it."

"What about you?"

"It's still not, well, perfect."

"And what would 'perfect' be?"

"I'm not sure. . . ."

"That customer liked it. I've been managing this department for a half-dozen years, and I've never before heard a customer say anything, good or bad, about a counter display. She's the person you have to please. You've pleased her. That pleases me. Therefore, the counter is finished. Congratulations."

"But . . ."

"Listen to your customers—they know best."

ISC
RESPONSIVE AND THOUGHTFUL

With high I, S, and C, your response to the focus situation is combining strong elements of the Influence, Supportiveness, and Conscientiousness dimensions.

Your ISC response pattern means that for you, the most satisfying part of this situation is the chance to get involved in a project and help others. Interaction is important to you; without it, work seems tough and unsatisfying. The people you work with appreciate your support, your willingness to make the best of things, and your meticulous attention to detail.

While you do not enjoy working alone in this situation, you don't see yourself as the leader. You prefer to work behind the scenes. While you don't want to be the star up on the stage, you like being part of the crew that makes it possible for the show to go on.

Value to the Group

You are comfortable in a cooperative environment in which people are usually pleasant and trusting of one another. In such a workplace, you'll be an active player.

You encourage others in tough times. You take into consideration their suggestions, requirements, and needs while doing your own work. You also pay close attention to the details of tasks.

In this situation, people probably don't expect you to take a leadership role, and they may look surprised when you speak up on an issue. When you do talk, though, they listen, for they know you have thought things through. People have found your insights worth hearing. You have a good track record.

ISC Style

What motivates you?

- Interacting with and supporting others
- Contributing to projects that require attention to detail
- Being appreciated for your willingness to make the best of a situation

What discourages you?

- Responsibility for leading others
- Working alone
- Having to speak up on behalf of your personal needs or interests

What is your favorite environment?

- Comfortable and cooperative
- Pleasant and trusting
- Opportunities to encourage others

What do you avoid?

- Responsibility for major decisions
- Risks
- Not having the time to think matters over on your own

Areas of Misunderstanding

Some people may think you're indecisive. The reality is that you need to consider all the pros and cons before making a decision—but you do make a decision when you're ready! You may want to let other know that you don't like to be rushed to a decision. When scheduling a project, try to reserve the time you need.

Information to Share

It may be difficult for you to share *any* information at all! You don't readily talk about your needs and wants. In fact, you probably look friendly and cheerful even when you aren't happy. Your colleagues, as well as your subordinates and your bosses, may act in ways you don't like at all without even realizing that they're doing it.

It will be well worth it for you to speak up on issues that are important to you. You might begin by talking about *positive* issues. From time to time, talk about what you like best about the work situation:

- how much you enjoy being on the team
- the satisfaction you feel when you make a contribution
- how good you feel when the team succeeds

You might want to share that you like playing a supporting role. Other people may take it for granted that *everyone* wants to be in the spotlight. When tasks are divvied up at the start of the project, bid for the supporting and behind-the-scenes work. You'll probably find that a number of people are pleased that you actually like that role.

What to Look Out For

Ironically, your reluctance to create conflict can become a source of conflict. If you present yourself as accommodating no matter how you really feel about a situation, sooner or later you will become frustrated and unsatisfied. Frustration and dissatisfaction never create harmony. If you think that speaking up is selfish, think about it some more. Your willingness to let others make decisions and your tendency to follow their direction without comment or objection may keep you from bringing crucial concerns and ideas to the attention of others.

Most likely, the group will benefit from your insights, because you are a careful observer and a thoughtful analyst.

When you speak up, focus on issues rather than personalities. For example, Pete proposes closing the office early next Friday. You realize that a new product is shipping earlier in the week and that customers probably will need support with installation and other questions. If you keep quiet about this, you may contribute to the creation of some dissatisfied, frustrated customers. If you voice your objection by beginning, "Pete, your idea won't work," you will likely spark conflict with Pete, because you seem to be attacking him personally. The most useful course is to focus on the issue: "We need to remember that Product X is launching Tuesday, and by Friday customers may be phoning in with questions and start-up problems." Don't tell Pete he's wrong. Let the group, including Pete, recognize the possible problems with the proposal.

A second possible area of conflict is your pace. You have a methodical, deliberate style and prefer to think through a problem before embarking on a course of action. Some people may become frustrated if they want to move faster than you.

Getting Unstuck
Situation: Your boss called you indecisive.
Possibility: You just need to think things through. Share your process.

Situation: You rarely speak up.

Possibility: You have such valuable insights. You need to share them.

Your Bottom Line

You are the kind of team member who makes it pleasant to work together on a project. You follow through on details. You keep up everyone's spirits. You think through problems, and when you are given the opportunity to do so, you generate important insights.

This Combination in Action

Sometimes the toughest thing to get from a boss is not a raise, but time—the time you need to think through a project, to analyze it, and to come up with a good plan.

Thomas is a customer-service and sales trainer who tends to respond to the beginning of a new project with an ISC response pattern. He's proud that he reacts that way, and he knows that he'll spend the time wisely. I asked him how he makes it work for him. He suggested the following tactics for successfully buying the time you need.

"Bosses, even the most understanding bosses, hate excuses, and they always tend to see a request to extend a deadline as a big bundle of excuses.

"Now, you might be able to get bosses to accept your excuses, but you will never be able to get them to like them. For this reason, it is best not to make excuses at all. Instead, recognize that extending a deadline is *buying* time, and like anything else you might purchase, the buying of time is subject to negotiation.

"Here's how I go about it. First I try to persuade the boss to 'sell' me more time in exchange for the greater value I can deliver: 'To do the most thorough job possible on this project, I'm going to need a week more. I don't think it will do us any good to try to rush it and end up neglecting x, y, and z.'

"I don't beg. I don't apologize. Above all, I don't make excuses. I just make it very clear what the additional time will buy, namely, a more thorough, more satisfactory job.

"Another important step is to keep your boss informed. Advise her as soon as any scheduling problem crops up. No one likes to feel backed into a corner, and showing that you are on top of the schedule shows that you are still in control, even if the deadline slips.

"After dangling the payoff, give your boss as many alternatives as possible: 'I can get x done by Wednesday, y by Friday, and z by early next week.' Or: 'If I put off x until next week, I can get you y and z by the scheduled deadline.' Avoid leaving your boss without choices, and you'll have a much better chance of getting the time you need.

"Above all, present the time increase as a change of schedule, not as a crisis."

The Research behind DiSC

In taking the DiSC profile in *I'm Stuck, You're Stuck,* you have joined the more than 40 million people worldwide who have used Inscape Publishing's DiSC products. Our DiSC products are based on the work of William Moulton Marston, Ph.D., as published in 1928 in his book *The Emotions of Normal People.* Marston set out to learn if there were systematic ways in which people responded to their environment. He was interested not only in how people behaved, but in how their behavior changed from situation to situation. Through his research, he hoped to increase people's understanding of themselves and others while decreasing misunderstandings. He found that two kinds of perception are particularly useful for explaining people's response in a particular situation: perception of environment and perception of one's self. As Marston observed, these two kinds of perception interact to describe an individual's response to a situation.

Dominance: When the environment is perceived as *unfavorable* and the person feels *more powerful* than the environment, he or she experiences a Dominant response. The person will likely try to change, fix, or control the situation.

Influence: When the environment is perceived as *favorable* and the person feels *more powerful* than the environment, he or she experiences a desire to Influence. The person will likely try to bring others around to his or her point of view.

Supportiveness: When the environment is perceived as *favorable* and the person feels *less powerful* than the environment, he or she experiences an opportunity to be Supportive. The person will likely try to keep the situation as it is and support those in need.

Conscientiousness: When the environment is perceived as *un-favorable* and the person feels *less powerful* than the environment, he or she responds with Conscientiousness. The person will likely set clear rules within the situation and work very hard to follow them.

Ongoing Research

While Marston created the DISC model, he never developed an instrument by which to measure it. For more than thirty years, Inscape Publishing has researched and refined the original DISC theory to maximize its impact and accuracy. Like our other recent DiSC products, the DiSC instrument in this book is based on our current research.

The first thing to consider when examining the research behind an instrument is the type of people who participated in the research, in other words, the sample. The sample determines for whom the instrument is appropriate. For example, if the sample were white male accountants from Kansas, then the instrument would be appropriate only for use by white male accountants from Kansas. Inscape Publishing made sure that our research sample was representative of people of different ages and racial backgrounds and from a wide variety of occupations and geographical locations. In other words, we made sure that our research sample represented you so that the instrument and feedback in *I'm Stuck, You're Stuck* would be helpful to you.

Next to be considered is the instrument's reliability and its validity. Reliability indicates whether a scale is measuring a construct (i.e., a concept such as dominance) *consistently*. Reliabilities are determined using a statistic called Cronbach's alpha coefficient. Scale reliabilities must be equal to or greater than .70 in order for a scale to be acceptable for use. Scale reliability coefficients for the DiSC instrument in *I'm Stuck, You're Stuck* range from .77 to .85.

Validity is whether a scale measures *what it is said to measure*. Validity was emphasized in creating both the scales and the response pattern feedback. The validity of the scales is supported by two types of statistical analyses, one called factor analysis and the other called multidimensional scaling. The feedback provided in *I'm Stuck, You're Stuck* is also based on research and thus follows closely the actual responses of persons who obtain a similar profile rather than being the "best guess" of the publisher.

Inscape Publishing's products are known for the sound research used to create and validate them. Our DiSC products are also distinctive in that they capture the situational nature of people's responses. All situations are not alike. As situations vary, so do our responses. The extensive research used to create Inscape Publishing's DiSC products allows the products to capture the differences in our responses from one situation to another. This, in turn, allows the respondent to capitalize on the full range of responses available to them as they pursue their goals and seek a better understanding of themselves.

Appropriate Use

People for whom the instrument is appropriate are individuals eighteen years and older who are interested in learning more about themselves. A seventh-grade reading level is necessary to fully understand both the response items and pattern interpretation.

The main purpose of the instrument is to assist individuals on their own path of human growth and discovery. We believe "you are the expert on you." We assume people are capable of setting their own goals, directing their efforts, and appraising results. We advise people to read their feedback and consider it carefully. After doing so, people are encouraged to make use of the information they find helpful and to disregard the information that is not.

Neither this book nor the instrument it contains is meant to be a substitute for mental health services. It is assumed that those completing the DiSC profile are in reasonably sound mental health, because no interpretations are available that would offer guidance in dealing with significant emotional issues. Persons seeking mental health counseling should obtain that help from a licensed counselor or therapist.

Additional DiSC Tool

good listener		want to make the rules	
put up with things I don't like		go straight ahead with projects	
willing to follow orders		act in a forceful way	
will go along with others		want to win	
think of others before I decide		will be the first to act	
willing to help		do not give in	
understand others' feelings		people see me as powerful	
nice to other people		sure of myself	
have warm feelings for people		want to be in charge	
let others lead		like to take action	
don't like to cause problems		quick to act	
don't make demands of people		feel strong	
Total column 1		**Total column 2**	
Subtract	-1	Add	+2
Score	●	Score	■